IGCSE ECONOMICS SIMPLIFIED

REVISION BOOK FOR GRADE 9 & 10

DR AMIT JOSHI

"This book is dedicated to my teachers, whose wisdom and guidance have shaped my journey, instilling in me the values of knowledge, perseverance, and curiosity. To my colleagues, whose support, collaboration, and shared passion for education have inspired me to grow both personally and professionally. To my family, whose unwavering love, patience, and encouragement have been my pillar of strength throughout this journey. And above all, to my students, who are my greatest motivation—your enthusiasm, inquisitiveness, and determination remind me every day of the true purpose of education. You inspire me to keep learning, evolving, and striving to make a difference."

Contents

Foreword

IGCSE Economics Simplified is a comprehensive, structured, and easy-to-understand guide designed to help students develop a strong foundation in economics. This book aims to simplify complex concepts, providing a clear and engaging learning experience that empowers students to think critically, apply economic principles, and excel in their IGCSE exams.

Written by Dr. Amit Joshi, a distinguished educator with over two decades of teaching experience, this guide reflectshis expertise in breaking down intricate economic theories into simplified, relatable ideas. His ability to connecteconomic principles with real-world applications ensures that students gain both theoretical knowledge and practical insights—a key requirement for mastering IGCSE Economics.

Whether you are struggling to understand core economic concepts or looking for a structured revision companion, this book serves as a one-stop resource to help students grasp essential topics, practice with real-life case studies, and develop analytical skills necessary for exam success.

Key Features of the Book

√? Concepts Made Simple & Engaging

This book is crafted to simplify economic concepts, ensuring that students can easily understand and retain key principles. Each topic is presented in a step-by-step format, breaking down complex theories into easy-to-grasp explanations.

√ Exam-Focused Approach

Aligned with the IGCSE Economics syllabus, this guide covers all major topics, including:

- The Basic Economic Problem
- Demand & Supply Mechanics
- Market Structures & Price Determination
- Macroeconomic Indicators (Inflation, GDP, Employment)
- Government Policies & Their Economic Impact
- Global Trade, Exchange Rates & Economic Development

√? Real-World Applications & Case Studies

To bridge the gap between theory and practical learning, this book includes numerous case studies and real-life examples to help students connect economics with real-world scenarios. This approach enhances critical thinking and ensures that students understand why economics matters in daily life.

Step-by-Step Exam Strategies

Scoring high in IGCSE Economics requires structured responses and analytical reasoning. This book provides exam-style questions, model answers, and answer-writing techniques to help students develop a clear and logical approach to answering exam questions.

√ Diagrams, Charts & Visual Aids for Better Understanding

Economics often involves graphs, tables, and statistical data interpretation. This book includes well-illustrated diagrams, flowcharts, and mind maps to aid visual learners and enhance comprehension.

√? Practice Questions & Self-Assessment Tools

Each chapter includes graded exercises, multiple-choice questions, short-answer questions, and data-response tasks to reinforce learning and track progress effectively.

√? Designed for Self-Study & Classroom Use

This guide is suitable for self-paced learning, group discussions, and classroom teaching, making it an ideal resource for both students and education.

Preface

Dr Amit Joshi

Dr. Amit Joshi is a distinguished educator, researcher, and facilitator with over two decades of teaching experience at both school and college levels. He holds a master's in business management, a doctorate in English, and postgraduate degrees in Commerce, English, and Economics. Currently serving as a Senior School Economics Teacher at Gandhi Memorial Intercontinental School, Jakarta, he is widely recognized for his ability to break down complex concepts into simple, easily comprehensible ideas, ensuring that students of all backgrounds can grasp intricate subjects with confidence. His expertise lies in making economics and interdisciplinary studies more accessible, fostering critical thinking, and instilling a passion for learning among his students.

A firm believer in experiential learning, Dr. Joshi integrates real-world applications into his teaching, bridging the gap between theory and practice. By employing innovative methodologies, interactive discussions, and case-based learning, he creates an engaging classroom environment that nurtures analytical and problem-solving skills.

As a prolific author and researcher, Dr. Joshi has made significant contributions to the academic community, with over 1,000 citations in various scholarly works. His publications, including research papers, case studies, and books, have been well-received in the fields of economics, commerce, and education. He also serves as a reviewer for several Scopus-indexed journals, further solidifying his role as a thought leader in his domain.In addition to his teaching and research, Dr. Joshi is an examiner for board papers, ensuring high academic standards in assessments and evaluations. His passion for mentoring students extends beyond the classroom, as he actively collaborates with them on researchprojects, guiding them toward academic excellence and publication in reputable journals.

With a deep commitment to education, research, and innovation, Dr. Amit Joshi continues to inspire students and educators alike, leaving a lasting impact on the academic community

ONE

PAPER FORMAT OF IGCSE ECONOMICS

Candidates must write two papers.

Paper 1 – Multiple Choice Duration: 45 minutes Max Marks: 30 marks

The Candidates answer all 30 multiple-choice questions. Candidates indicate their answers on the multiple- choiceanswer sheet provided questions are based on all six sections of the syllabus content. The questions may include calculations. Calculators may be used in the examination.

The paper assesses the following assessment objectives: AO1: Knowledge and understanding AO2: Analysis **Paper 2 – Structured Questions** Duration: 2 hours 15 minutes Max Marks: 90 marks

Candidates answer one compulsory question in Section A and three questions from a choice of four in Section

Candidates should be aware of the marks for each part question. These are printed on the question paper. Use them as a guide to the amount of detail and length of response expected and to help them manage their time effectively.Calculators may be used in both sections of the examination.

PAPER 2: Structure and Guidelines

Paper 2 consists of two sections. Section A includes one case study worth 20 marks, divided into six questions.Each question is structured around a specific command term, which determines the depth of the response required. Marks are awarded accordingly.

To maximize your score, follow these structured suggestions and answering techniques:

1a [2 marks] – DEFINE

This question requires a precise definition of an economic term or a simple calculation.

For definitions: Provide the exact definition as learned from the textbook. Do not elaborate or provide examples unless specifically asked.

For calculations: Show the method used to arrive at the answer. The correct formula and steps contribute to 1 mark, while the final correct answer with appropriate units carries another mark.

1b [2 marks] – IDENTIFION

This question requires you to identify two products, concepts, or situations from the given case study. No explanation is required—simply state the correct terms as found in the source.

Ensure that your answers are directly derived from the case study.

1c [2 marks] – EXPLAIN

You will be asked to explain one reason or effect based on the provided case study.

Structure your response as follows:

1 mark for correctly identifying the reason/effect from the text.

1 mark for explaining how it impacts the situation.

Keep your explanation concise and relevant to the case study.

1d [4 marks] – ILLUSTRATE/DRAW

This question requir es a labelled diagram to visually represent a concept.

Guidelines for drawing:Clearly label all cmponents.

Use arrws t indicate any changes (such as shifts in demand r supply curves).

No written explanation is needed unless explicitly requested.

1e [4 marks] – ANALYZE

This question assesses your ability to break down an economic concept and apply it to the case study.

Answer structure:

What: Define the concept.

Why: Explain the relationship or impact.

How: Support your answer with a relevant example from the case study.

Example: If the question asks about the relationship between price and quantity demanded, explain the inverse relationship, cite an example from the case study, and analyse why this occurs.

1f [6 marks] – DISCUSS

This question typically requires you to evaluate two sides of an argument (advantages vs. disadvantages).

Structure your response as follows:

Clearly explain WHAT the advantage/disadvantage is and HOW it impacts the situation.

Important: Avoid repeating the same argument in reverse form. Each point should be unique and well-explained.Final Tips for Success

- Always refer to the case study while answering.
- Keep answers concise yet complete—only elaborate when necessary.
- Use economic terminology correctly.
- Maintain clarity and logical structure in your responses.
- Practice past papers to get familiar with the format and improve time management.

PAPER 2: Section B – Structure and Answering Strategy

Overview

Section B consists of four different situations or pieces of information, each presented in paragraph form. Each situation is followed by four questions, each based on a specific command term. Marks are awarded based on thedepth and accuracy of responses.

To maximize your score, follow the structured suggestions and answering techniques outlined below:

2a [2 marks] – DEFINE

This question typically requires a precise definition of an economic term or a simple calculation.

For definitions: Provide the textbook definition without elaboration or examples unless explicitly required.

For calculations: Show the correct formula and method, with appropriate units.

Marks allocation :

1 mark for the correct definition/formula.

1 mark for the correct final answer (with units, if applicable).

2a [2 marks] – IDENTIFY

You will be asked to identify two products, concepts, or situations directly from the given case study.

No explanation is required—simply state the correct terms as found in the source.

Ensure that answers are derived directly from the case study.

2b [4 marks] – EXPLAIN

This question requires you to explain two reasons, effects, or consequences based on the case study.

Structure your response as follows:

1 mark per crrect identificatin f the reasn/effect. 1 mark per explanatin detailing its impact

Example Structure:

Point 1: Identify the reason (1 mark) → Explain the impact (1 mark).

Point 2: Identify anther reason (1 mark) → Explain its impact (1 mark).

Keep the explanation clear, logical, and relevant to the case study.

2c [6 marks] – ANALYZE

This question assesses your ability to break down an economic concept and apply it to the case study.

Structure your response as follows:

Para 1: Intrduction – Define key ecnomic terms related t the questin (only if nt already defined in an earlier part).

Para 2: Identificatin – Relate the questin t the infrmation prvided in the case study.

Para 3: A nalysis – Explain what will happen, why it will happen, and hw it will happen. Use:

   What: Define the economic relationship.

Why: Explain the cause of the change.

How: Provide an example or a diagram (if required) to support your analysis.

If a diagram is required, ensure:

- It is labelled correctly.
- Arrows indicate any shifts.
- Changes in equilibrium are clearly marked.

Example Analysis:

If analysing a demand shift, explain hw factrs like incme changes impact cnsumer purchasing power,leading to a shift in the demand curve.

2d [8 marks] – DISCUSS

The command term "discuss" means providing a balanced and well-reasoned evaluation of an economic concept.

You must present both sides of the arguments:

Advantages (3 points)

Disadvantages (2 points) OR vice versa (2 advantages, 3 disadvantages).

Use ecnomic concepts, terminlogy, and data t supprt yur respnse.The discussion may also explore uncertainties related to different outcomes or alternative decisions. Answer Structure:Para 1: IntroductionDefine key economic terms related to the question.Instead of listing definitions separately, integrate them into a coherent introduction (like an essay).If possible, provide a real-world example.

Para 2: Diagram (if applicable) to Draw a labelled diagram if the question requires or benefits from visual representation.

Para 3: Explanation

Explain the diagram and connect it to the given case study information.

Para 4: Arguments in Favoro State 2-3 supporting arguments and explain how they justify the economic decision or outcome.

Para 5: Counter arguments State 2-3 counterarguments that challenge the idea.

Para 6: Conclusion Based on your analysis, conclude whether the decision should or should not be implemented.

Justify your stance with logical reasoning.

Example Question & Answer Breakdown

Scenario:

Finland is a high-income country with a shortage of land and labour. It is often cited as an example of a market economy. However, the government intervenes by encouraging its population to eat two servings of fruit and vegetables per day.

Q. Explain how an increase in a worker's income can affect their mobility of labour. [4 marks]

Answer Structure:

Higher income allows workers to afford educatin (1 mark), which increases ccupational mobility (1 mark). Higher income makes housing more affordable (1 mark), which increases gegraphical mobility (1 mark). Higher income may also make workers reluctant to switch jobs due to jb satisfaction (1 mark), which could reduce mobility (1 mark). Higher inocme allows better access to transportation (1 mark), which increases gegraphical mobility (1 mark).

Q. Analyse, using a demand and supply diagram, how a greater awareness of the health benefits of eating fruit will affect the fruit market. [6 marks]

Answer:Diagram (4 marks)

Correctly labelled Price and Quantity axes (1 mark). Originaldemand and supply curves labelled (1 mark). New demand curve shifts right (1 mark). Equilibriums (P1, Q1 → P2, Q2) marked (1 mark).

Written Analysis (2 marks)

Greater awareness of health benefits increases demand for fruit (1 mark). This leads to higher prices and increased quantity traded (1 mark).

Q. Discuss whether a market economy benefits an economy. [8 marks]

Answer Structure:

Introduction:

Define market economy and provide an example. Diagram:Not required but could show market failure if applicable.

Arguments in Favor:

Profit incentive and competition increase efficiency. Wage differentials encourage effort.

Low prices and high quality due to competition. High consumer choice and sovereignty.

Counterarguments:

Market failure risks (e.g., externalities). Public goods may not be provided.

Monopoly power may arise.

High unemployment due to lack of coordination.

TWO
DIAGRAMS TO REMEMBER

1. Production Possibility curve

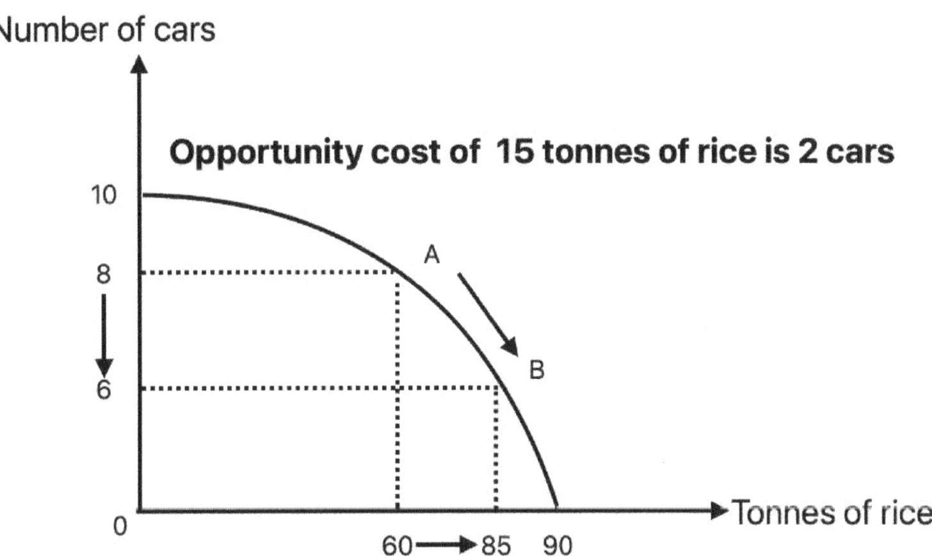

Fig 1: Production possibility curve

The concave shape (bowed outward) shows the Law of Increasing Opportunity Cost.As we shift resources from producing cars to rice, we give up more and more cars for additional rice.This happens because resources are not equally efficient in producing both goods (e.g., skilled car workers cannot easily switch to farming rice).

Moving along the PPC means choosing to produce more of one good while sacrificing some of the other. Example from the graph:At Point A → The ecnomy produces 60 tonnes of rice and 8 cars If we increase wheat to 85 tonnes (Point B), car production drops to 6. The opportunity cost of producing 25 extra tonnes of wheat is 2 cars.

2. Right shift of PPC [Economic Growth]

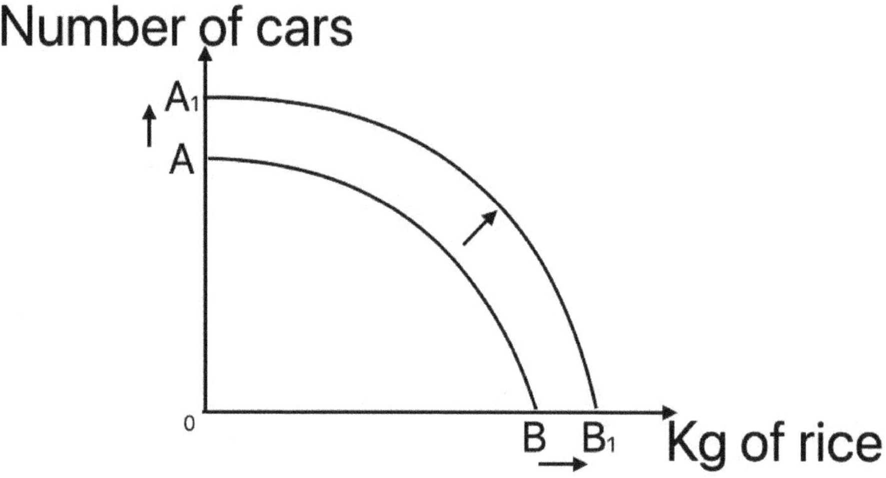

Fig 2: Right shift of PPC

The line PPC showin 'A' number of cars and 'B' kg of rice before economic growth. The PPC, shifts outward, showing that the economy can now produce more A1 units of cars and B1 kgs of rice.

3. Left shift of PPC [Economic Decline]

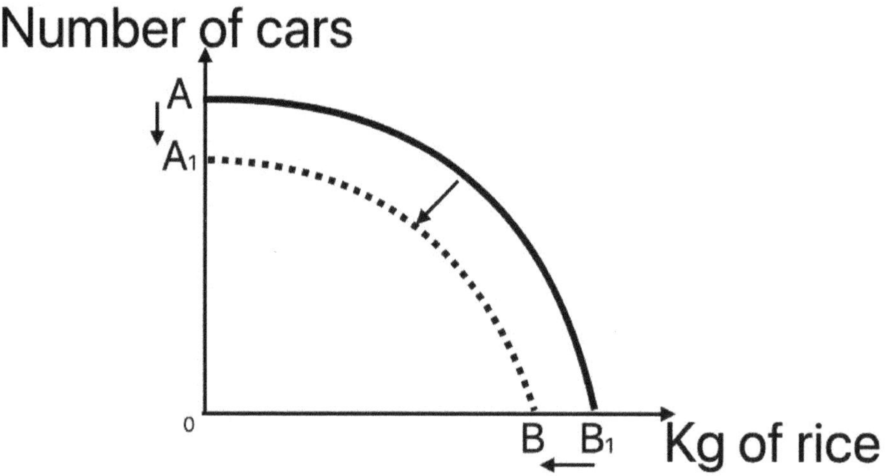

Fig 3: Left shift of PPC

A leftward shift of the PPC means that the economy's productive capacity has decreased, reducing the ability to produce both goods (rice and Cars). This represents economic decline or a reduction in resources. The bold curve is the original PPC before the decline. The dashed curve is the new PPC,shifted inward, showing that the economy can now produce less rice and fewer Cars than before.

4: **Points on, in and outside PPC**

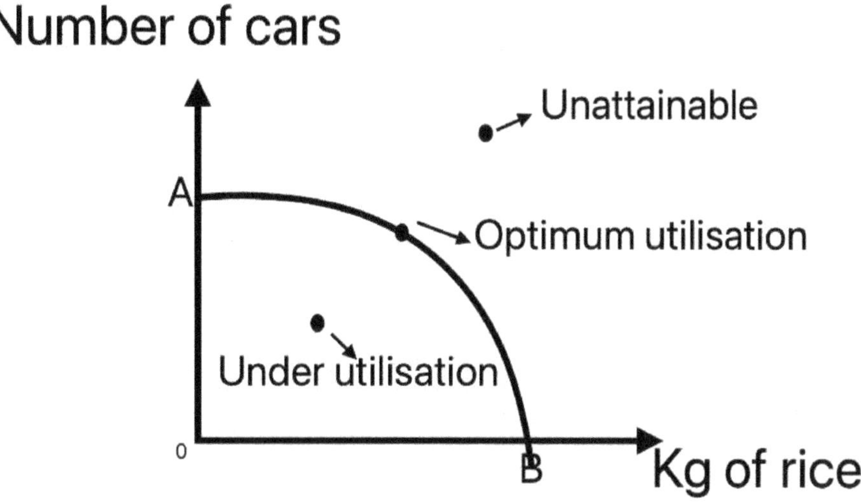

Fig 4: **Points on, in and outside PPC**

A Production Possibility Curve (PPC) shows the maximum combinations of two goods or services that can be produced given the available resources and technology. Points on, under, and beyond a PPC have different meanings. **Points on the PPC (B):** These represent efficient use of resources where the economy is producing the maximum possible output of two goods, given the resources available.Every point on the curve indicates full utilization of resources. **Points under the PPC (A) :** These represent inefficient use of resources, where the economy is not fully utilizing its resources, and more of both goods could be produced without sacrificing the production of either good. **Points beyond the PPC (C) :** These are unattainable with the current resources andtechnology.

5. Demand Curve

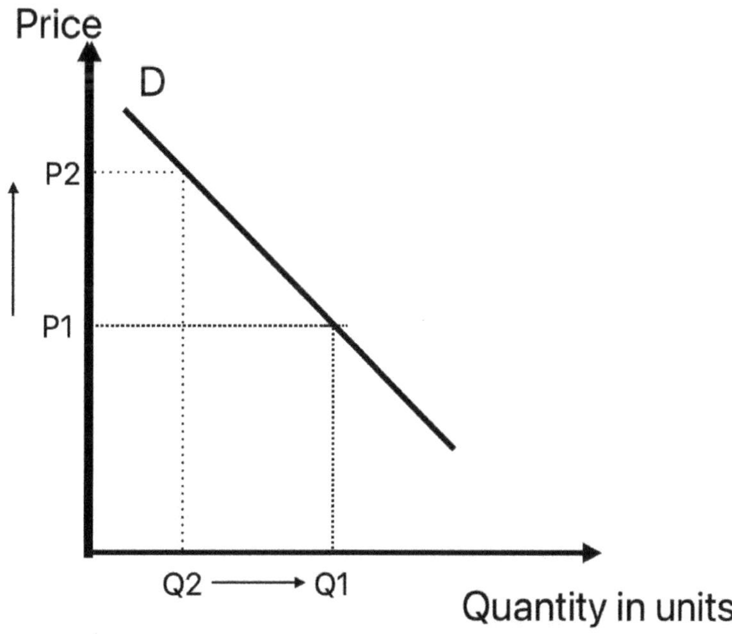

Fig 5: Demand curve

The **demand curve** slopes **downward** from left to right, indicating an **inverse relationship** between price and quantitydemanded as shown in the diagram. The x axis represents the quantity of good or service and y axis represent price of thegood or service. as price of cloth decreases from 10 pound to 8, quantity demanded increases from 10 meters to 20 meters. Similarly as the price further falls from 8 pounds to 6 , the quantity demanded increases from 20 meters to 40 meters. The 'D' represents downward sloping demand curve.

6. Extension in demand

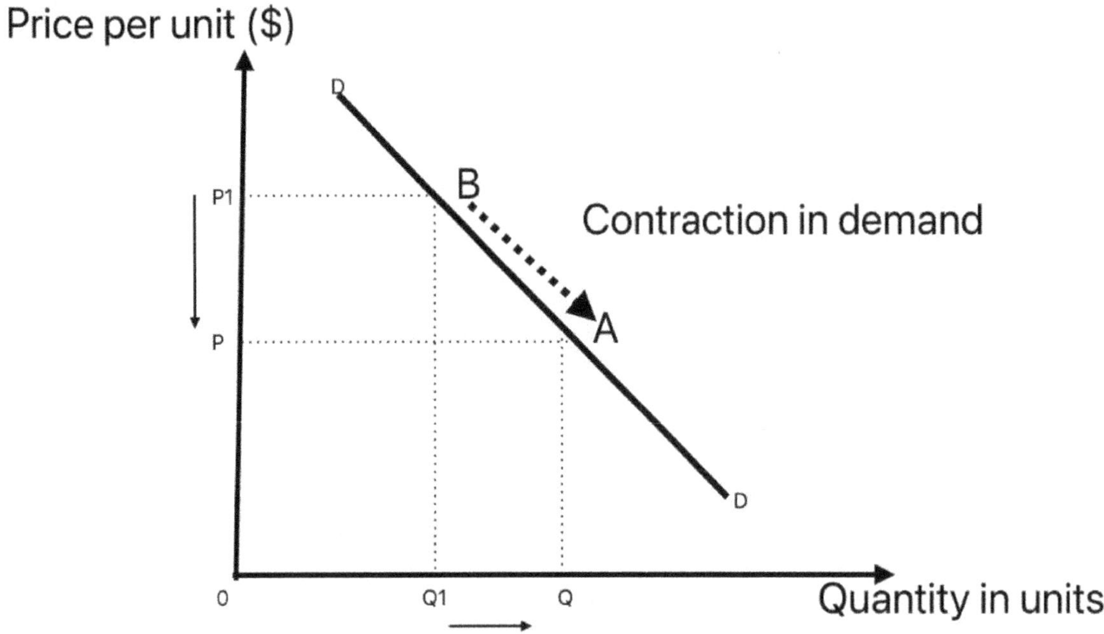

Fig 6: Extension in demand

An extension in demand refers to the increase in the quantity demanded due to a decrease in the price of a good or service while other factors remain constant (ceteris paribus). This concept follows the law of demand, which states that when the price of a product falls, its demand increases. The x-axis represents the quantitydemanded in units .The y-axis represents the price of good in rupees. The demand curve (DD) slopes downward from left to right, showing the inverse relationship between price and quantity demanded. When the price decreases Rs 20 to Rs 10, the quantity demanded increases from 5 units to 10 units. this movement along the demand curve from A to B represents an extension in demand.

7. Contraction in demand

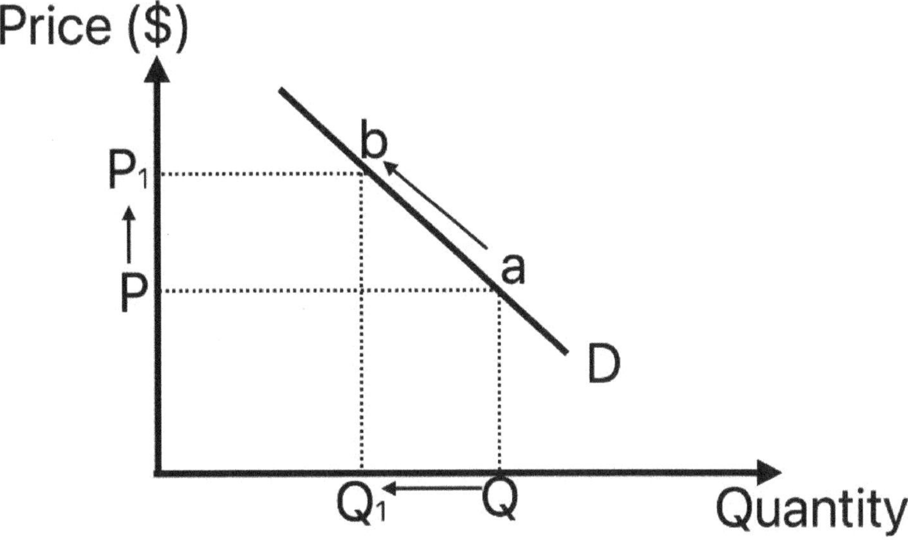

Fig 7: Contraction in demand

Contraction in demand refers to a decrease in the quantity demanded of a good or service due to an increase in its price, while other factors remain constant (ceteris paribus). It is represented as an upward movement along the demand curve. · The X-axis represents the quantity demanded .

The Y-axis represents the price of the good (P). The downward-sloping demand curve (D) shows the inverse relationship between price and quantity demanded.When price increases from P1 to P2, the quantity demanded contracts from D1 to D2, moving upwards along the demand curve.

8. Increase in demand

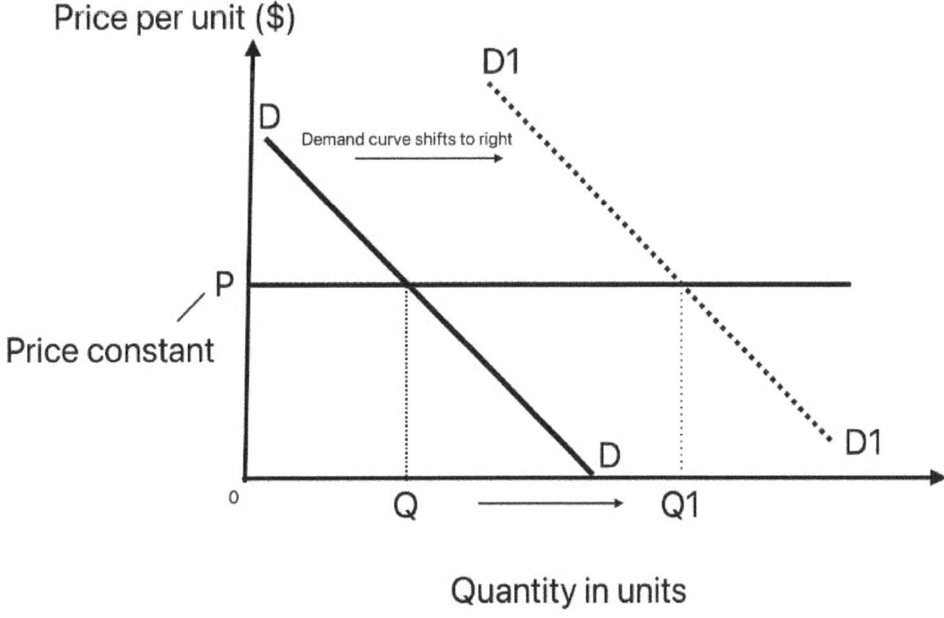

Fig 8: Increase in demand

An **increase in demand** occurs when consumers are willing to buy more of a good or service at every price level, shifting the demand curve **to the right**. The **initial demand curve** is labeled as **D**. Due to reasons other than price of the good, the demand curve shifts **rightward** to **D1**. At the same price **P** the quantity demanded increases from **Q to Q1**.This shift indicates that for the same price level, more units of the good are demanded.

9. Decrease in demand

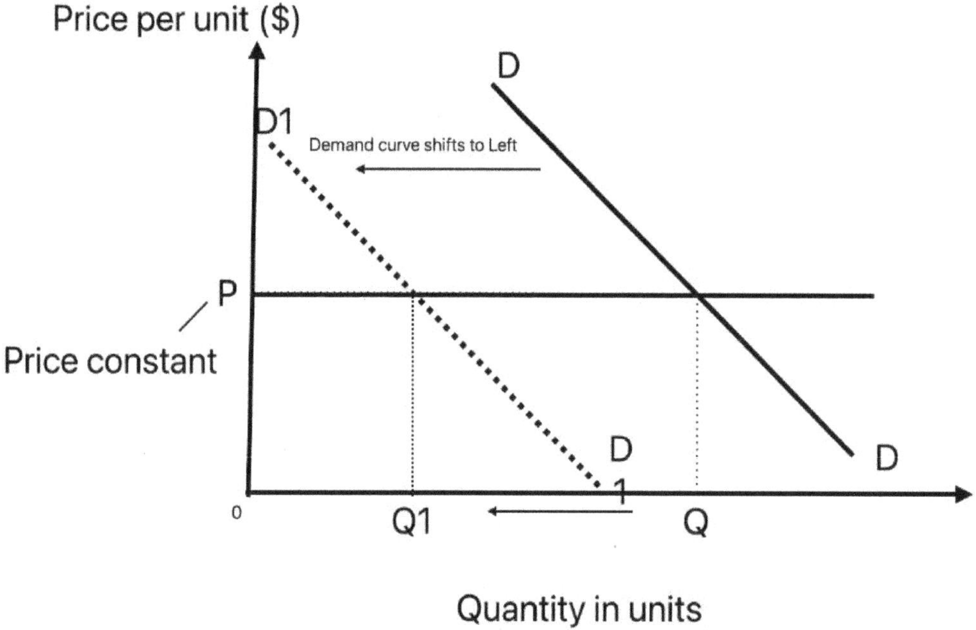

Fig 9: Decrease in demand

A decrease in demand occurs when consumers are willing to buy less of a good or service at every price level, shiftingthe demand curve to the left. This means that at the same price, the quantity demanded is lower than before. The initial demand curve is D (dotted line), Due to a decrease in demand, the demand curve shifts leftward to D1(solid line). At price 4$ initially 6 quantity was being demanded, at the same price demand falls to 4 units.

10. Market demand from individual demand

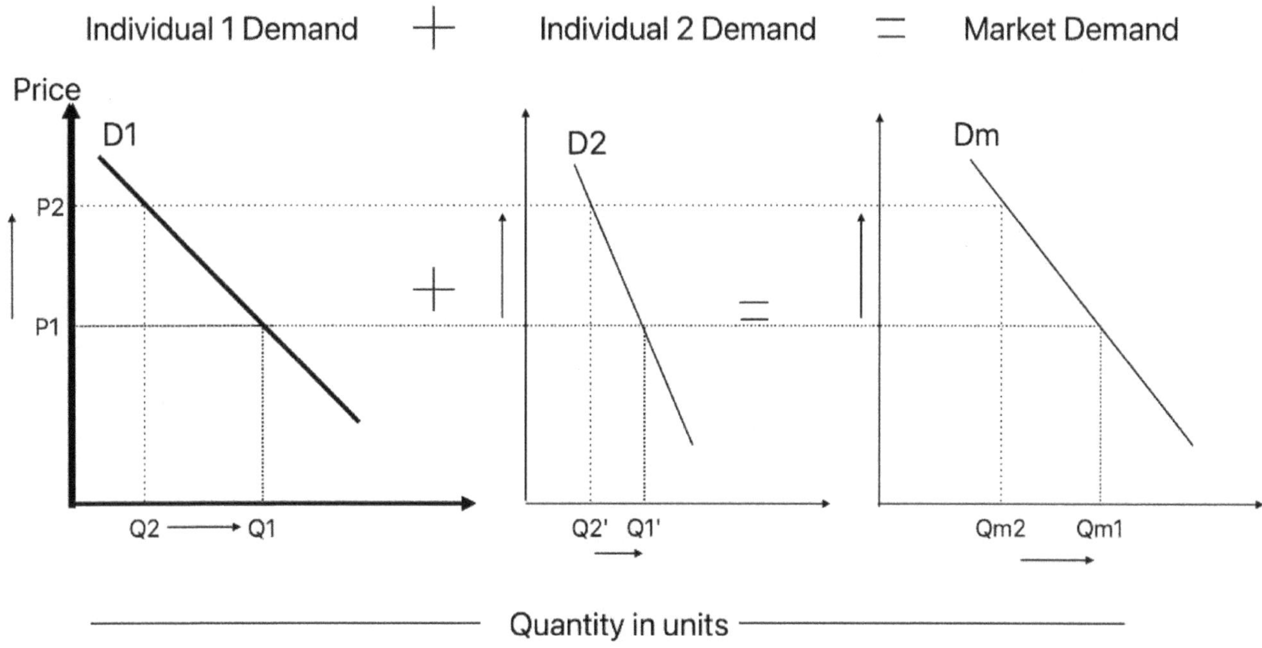

Fig 10: Market demand curve from individual demand curve

Market demand is the **total demand** for a good or service in an economy, derived by summing up the individual demands of all consumers at each price level. It represents the overall willingness and ability of allbuyers in the market to purchase a good at different prices. Consider **two consumers**, Individual 1 and individual 2. Each has their own individual demand curve. The market demand curve is found by summing the quantity demandedat each price level(Dm.The total quantity demanded from the market at P1 prive is the sum of individual demand at that prive [Qm1=Q1+Q1']. and market demand at P2 price is Qm2 which is sum of Q2 and Q2'.

11. Unit Price Elastic Demand [PED=1]

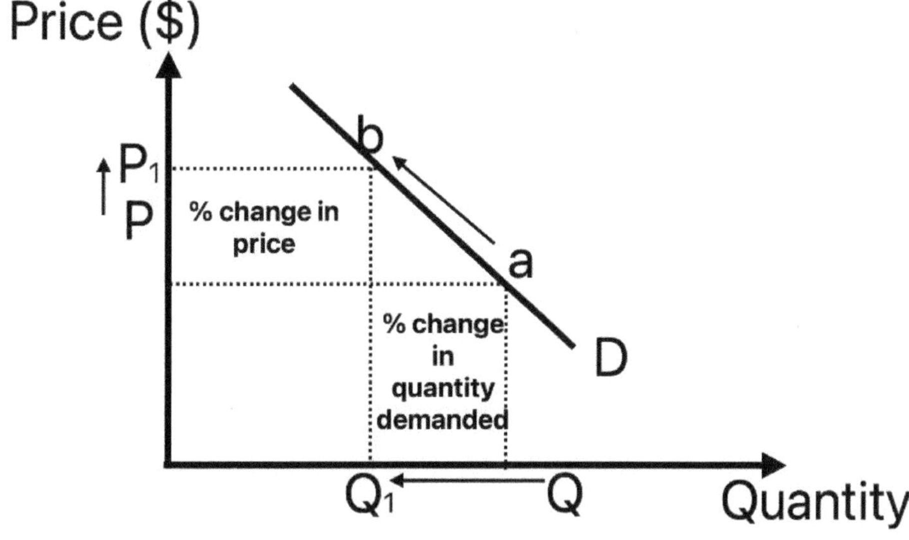

Fig 11: Unit price elastic demand

Unitary price elastic demand occurs when the percentage change in quantity demanded is exactly equal to the percentage change in price. This means that total revenue remains constant when the price changes.The demand curve (D) represents unitary elastic demand. If price increases from P to P1, the quantity demanded decreases by the same proportion from Q to Q1

12. Price elastic demand [PED>1]

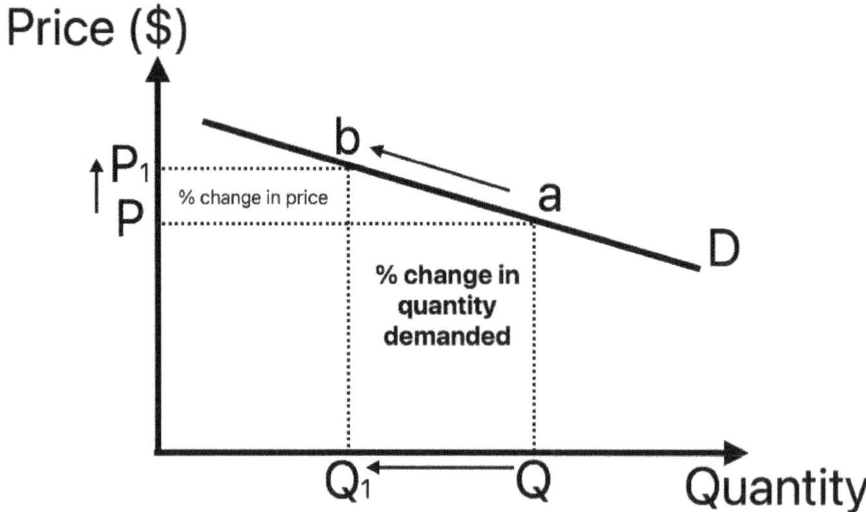

Fig 12: Price elastic demand

Relatively elastic demand occurs when a **small change in price leads to a larger change in quantity demanded**. This means that consumers are highly responsive to price changes. The **price elasticity of demand (Ed) > 1**, indicating that the percentage change in quantity demanded is greater than the percentage change in price. The demand curve (**D**) represents relatively elastic demand. A **small price increase** from **P1 to P2** leads to a **large decrease in quantity demanded** from **Q to Q1**.

13. Price inelastic demand PED<1

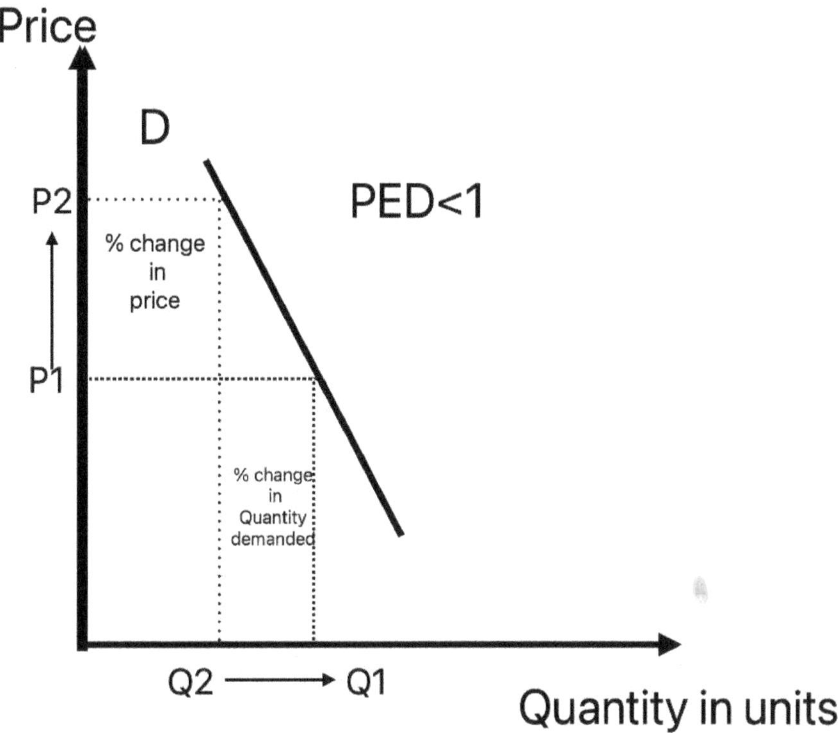

Fig 13: Inelastic demand

Relatively inelastic demand occurs when a **change in price leads to a smaller change in quantity demanded**. This means that consumers are **less responsive** to price changes. The **price elasticity of demand(Ed) < 1**, indicating that the percentage change in quantity demanded is **less** than the percentage change inprice. The demand curve (**D**) represents relatively inelastic demand. A **large price increase** from P1 **to P2** leads to a **small decrease in quantity demanded** from Q2 **to Q1**.

14. Perfectly inelastic demand [PED=0]

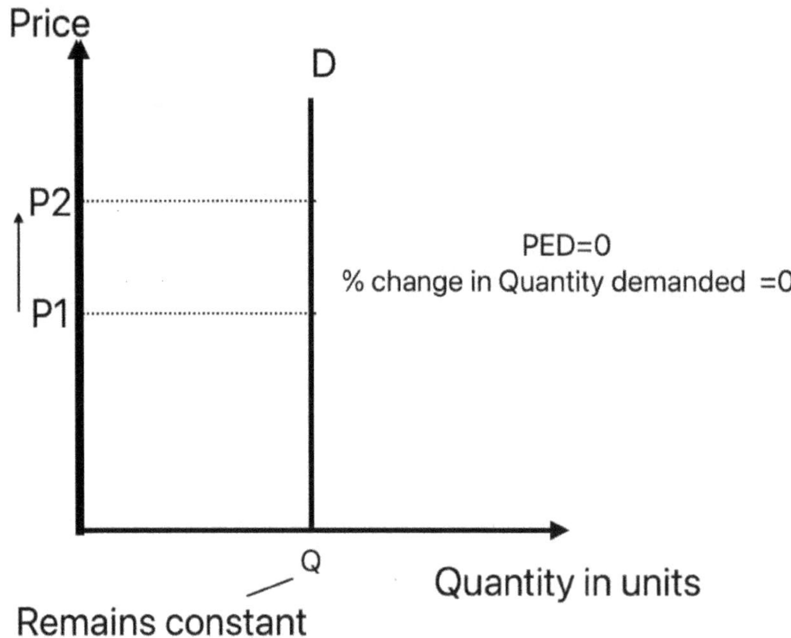

fig 14. Perfectly inelastic demand

Perfectly inelastic demand occurs when **a change in price has no effect on the quantity demanded**. Consumers will continue to buy the same amount of the good regardless of its price. The **price elasticit of demand (Ed) = 0**, meaning there is **zero responsiveness** to price changes. The demand curve (**D**) is **vertical**, indicating that **quantity demanded (Q)** remains **constant** regardless of the price level.Even if the price rises from P1 **to P2**, the quantity demanded stays the same (**Q**).

15. Perfectly price elastic demand [PED=Infinite]

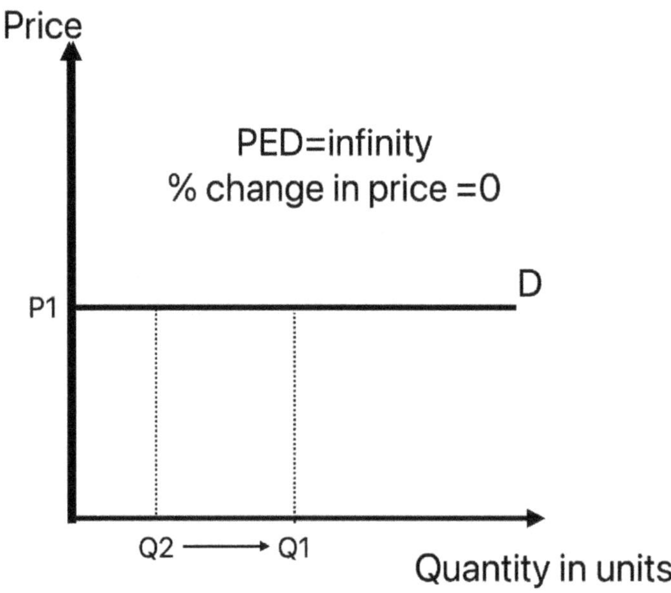

FIG 15: Perfectly price elastic demand

Perfectly elastic demand occurs when **even a tiny change in price leads to an infinite change in quantitydemanded**. Consumers will buy at only one specific price, and any increase in price will reduce demand to zero. The **price elasticity of demand (Ed) = ∞**, meaning demand is infinitely responsive to price changes. The demand curve (**D**) is **horizontal**, indicating that consumers will buy any amount of units at a fixed price (**P1**).

16. Law of supply

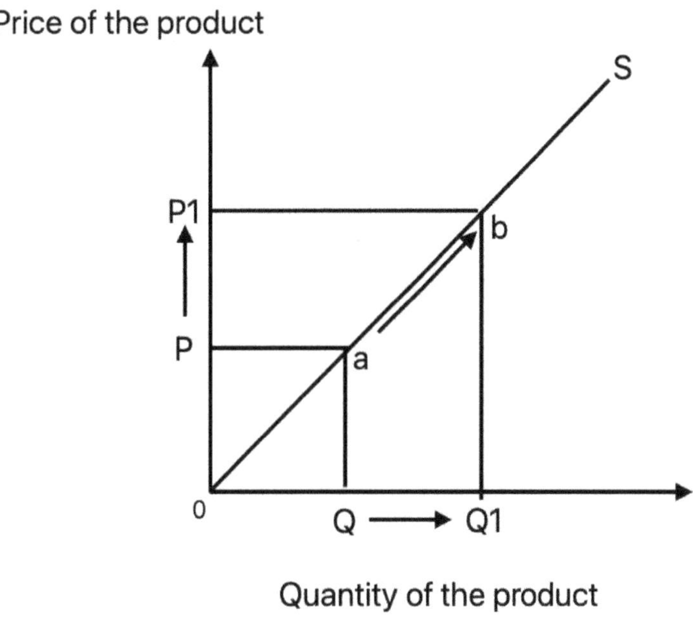

Fig 16: Relationship between price and quantity supplied

Other factors remaining constant, an increase in the price of a good or service leads to an increase in the quantity supplied, and a decrease in price leads to a decrease in quantity supplied. This occurs because higher prices provide greater incentives for producers to supply more, as it leads to higher potential profits. The supply curve (S) is upward sloping, showing the direct relationship between price (P) and quantity supplied(Q).As price increases from 6 to 12, the quantity supplied rises from 12 to 6.Conversely, if price falls, producers reduce supply.

17. Market supply curve

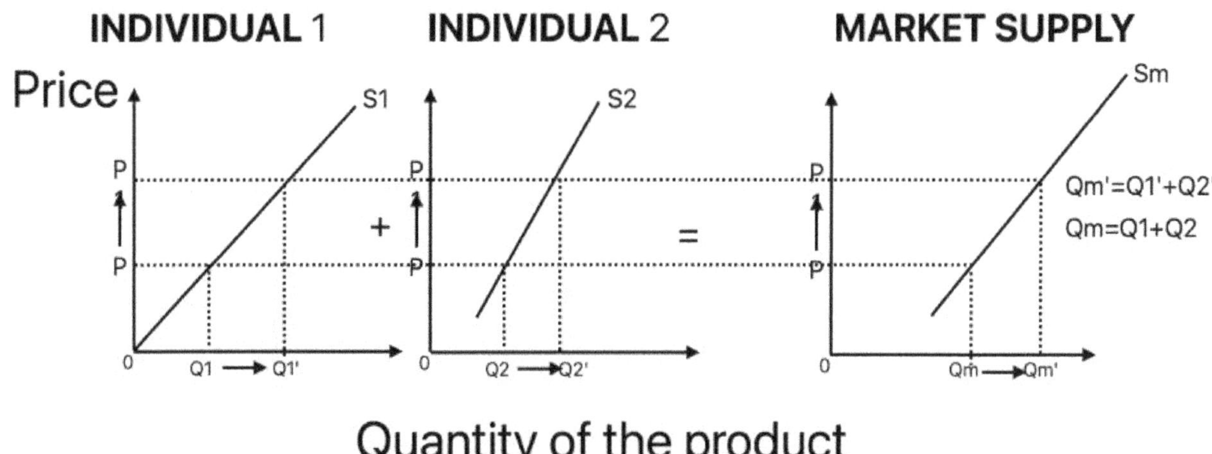

Fig 17: Market supply from individual supply

Market supply refers to the total quantity of a good or service that all producers in a market are willing and able to supply at different price levels over a given period, assuming all other factors remain constant (ceterisparibus). It is the sum of individual supplies of all firms producing the same good in the market. In the above diagram Producer 1 is supplyin Q1 units at P price and at the same price (P) individual 2 is supplying Q2 units. So the total supply in the market at 'P' price is Qm which is the sum of individual quantity supplied (Q1+Q2).

18. Extension in supply curve (increase in quantity demanded)

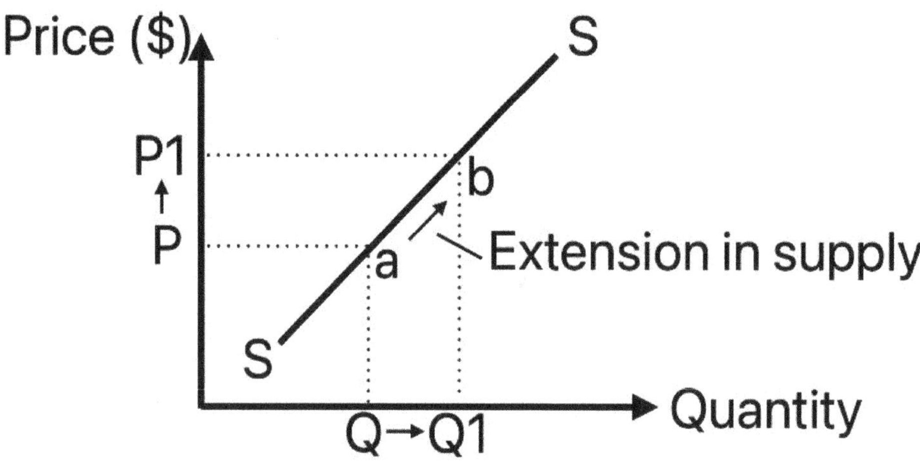

fig 18:Extension in supply curve

An extension in supply refers to an increase in the quantity supplied due to an increase in the price of a good or service, while other factors remain constant (ceteris paribus). It is represented by an upward movement along the supply curve rather than a shift of the curve itself.the supply curve (S) remains unchanged. As price increases from P to P1, the quantity supplied increases from Q to Q1. This movement along the same supply curve from a to b is called extension in supply.

19. Contraction in supply curve (decrease in quantity supplied)

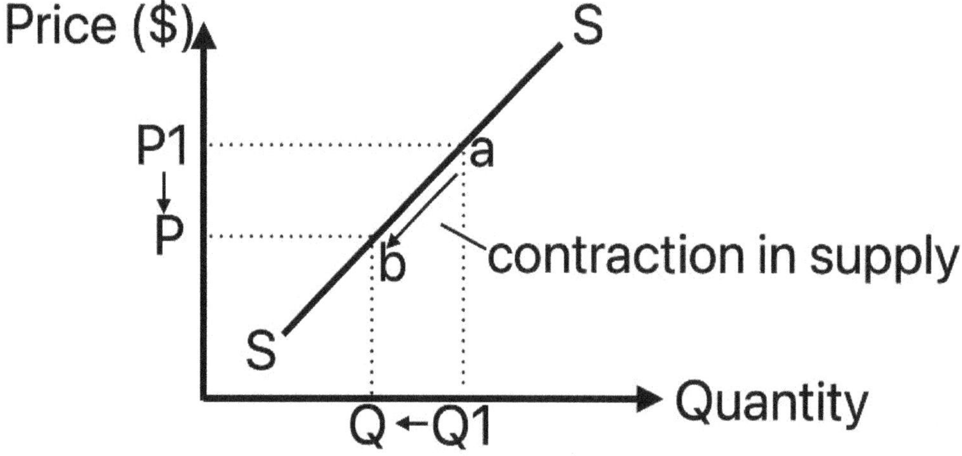

Fig 19:Contraction in supply curve

Fall in quantity supplied from Q1 to Q due to a fall in the price from P1 to P of a good or service, while other factors remain constant (ceteris paribus). It is represented by a downward movement along the supply curve,rather than a shift of the curve itself. The supply curve (S) remains unchanged. As price decreases from P1 to P, the quantity supplied decreases from Q1 to Q.This movement along the same supply curve from b to a is called contraction in supply.

20. Rightward shift of supply curve or increase in supply

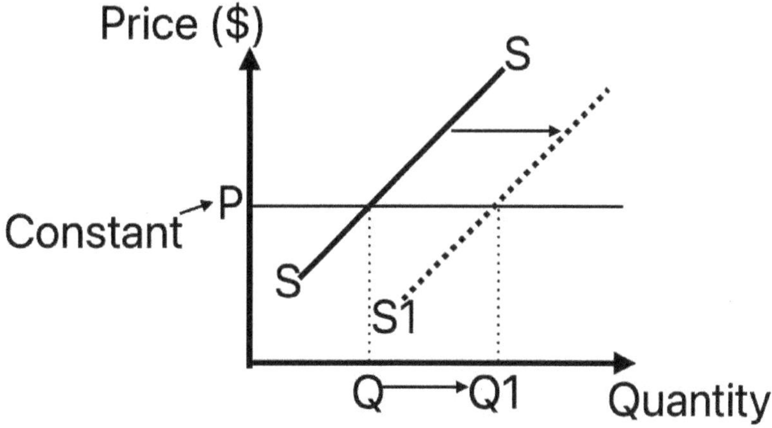

Fig 20: Increase in supply

An increase in supply refers to a situation where producers are willing to supply more of a good or service atthe same price due to favorable changes in non-price factors. This causes the supply curve to shiftrightward. The original supply curve is S.Due to favorable factors, the supply curve shifts rightward to S1. At the same price P, the quantity supplied increases from Q to Q1.

21. Leftward shift of supply curve or decrease in supply

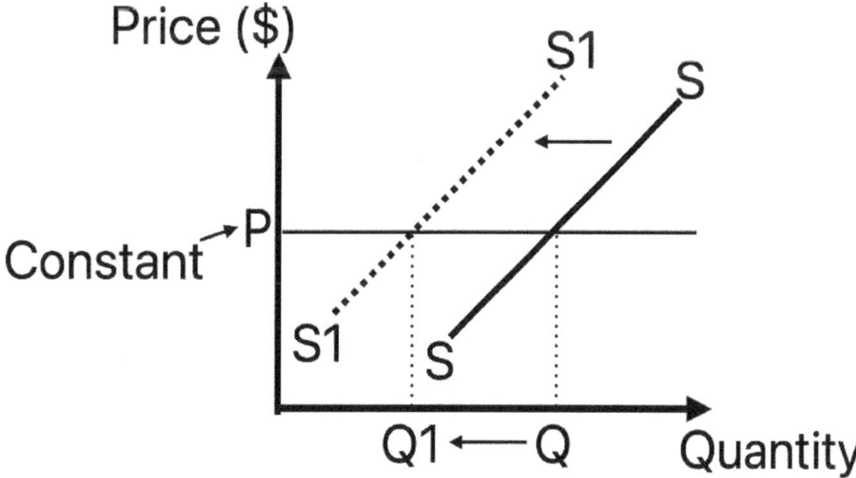

Fig 21: Decrease in supply

A decrease in supply refers to a situation where producers are willing to supply less of a good or service at the same price due to unfavorable changes in non-price factors. This causes the supply curve to shift leftward. The original supply curve is S.Due to unfavorable factors, the supply curve shifts leftward to S1. At the same price P, the quantity supplied decreases from Q to Q1.

22. Unit price elastic supply [PES=1]

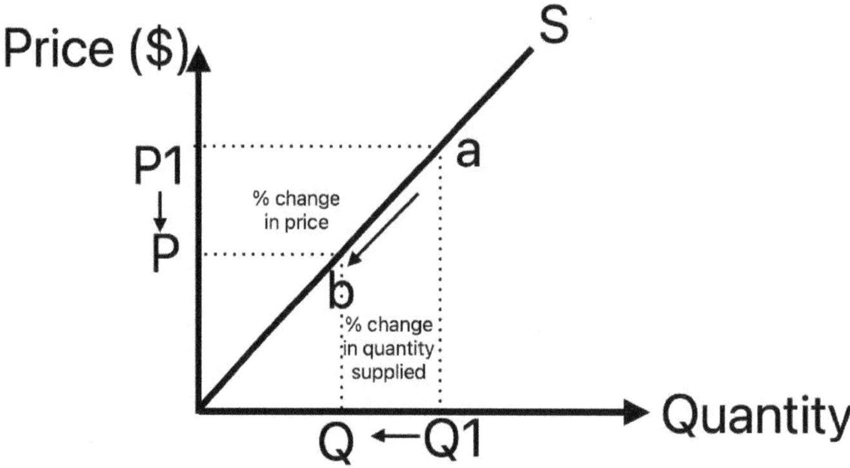

Fig 22: Unit price elastic supply

Unit elastic supply refers to a situation where the percentage change in quantity supplied is exactly equal to the percentage change in price. This means that the elasticity of supply (Es) is equal to 1. The supply curve (S)passes through the origin, showing that price and quantity move in direct proportion. If price decreases from P1 to P, quantity supplied decreases proportionally from Q1 to Q.

23. Price elastic supply [PES>1]

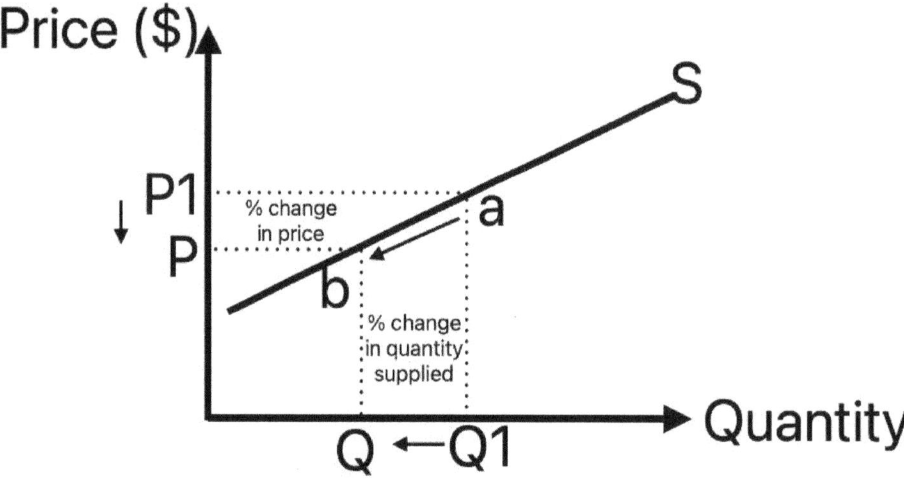

Fig 23: Price elastic supply

Relatively elastic supply refers to a situation where the percentage change in quantity supplied is greaterthan the percentage change in price. This means that the elasticity of supply (Es) is greater than 1.Thesupply curve (S) is relatively flatter.A small price decrease from P1 to P results in a large decrease in quantity supplied from Q1 to Q.[**Note: when extended touches y axis**].

24. Price inelastic supply [PES<1]

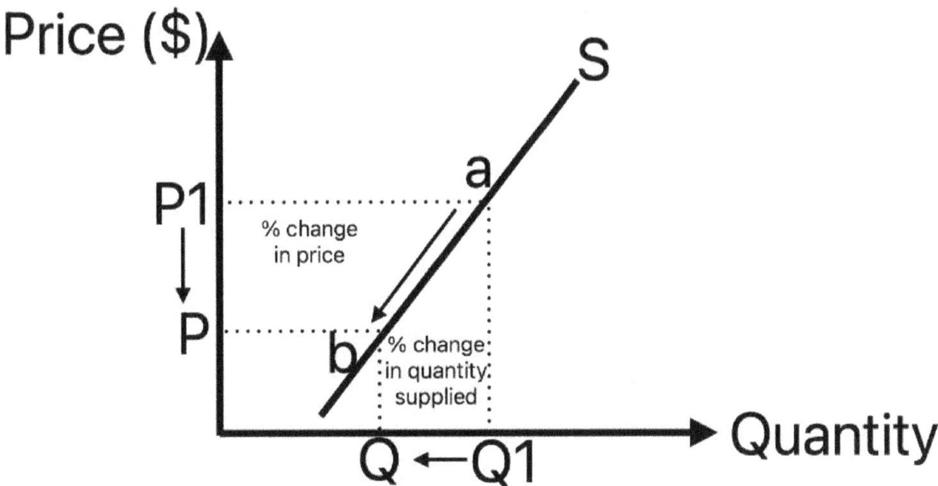

Fig 24: Price inelastic supply

Relatively inelastic supply occurs when the percentage change in quantity supplied is less than the percentage change in price. This means that the elasticity of supply (Es) is less than 1.The supply curve (S) is relatively steeper.(touches x axis if extended). A significant price decrease from 'P1' to P results in only a small decrease in quantity supplied from Q1 to Q.

25. Perfectly inelastic supply [PES=0]

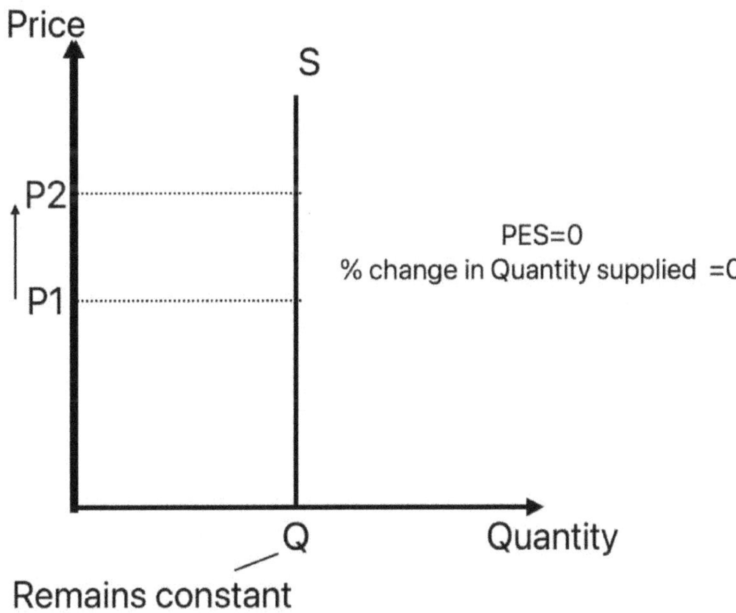

Fig 25: Perfectly inelastic supply

A perfectly inelastic supply curve is a vertical line, indicating that the quantity supplied remains constant regardless of the price. This situation occurs when suppliers cannot increase or decrease the quantity of a good, regardless of market price changes. In the above diagram price increases from P1 to P2, but the quantity supplied remains constant at Q.

26. Perfectly elastic supply [PES=infinite]

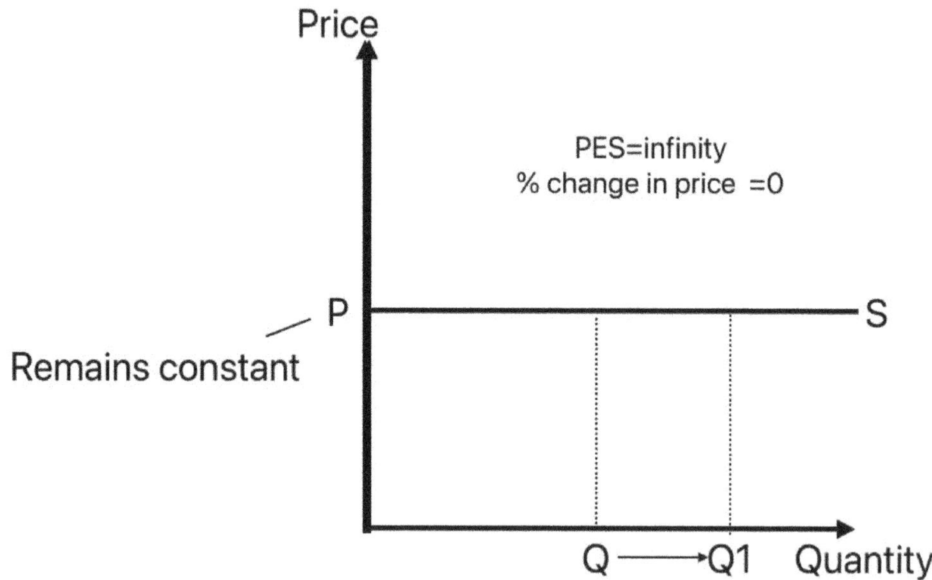

Fig 26: Perfectley elastic supply

Perfectly elastic supply refers to a situation where even the smallest change in price causes an infinitechange in quantity supplied. This means that the elasticity of supply (Es) is infinite. The supply curve (S) is horizontal at price P. At price P, producers are willing to supply any quantity (Q, Q1, Q2, etc.).

27. Market equilibrium in a free market

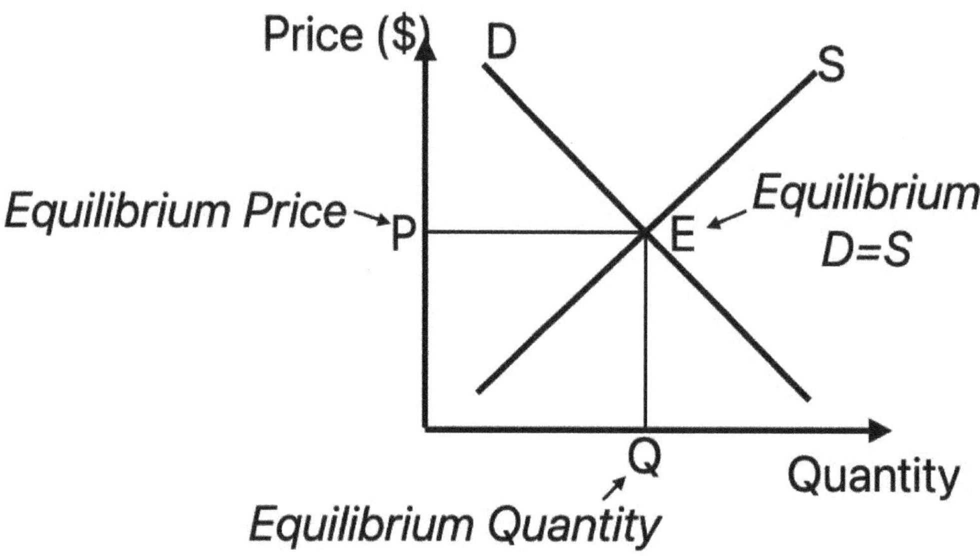

Fig 27: Market equilibrium

Market equilibrium is the point where the quantity demanded by consumers equals the quantity supplied by producers at a specific price. At this equilibrium price, there is no shortage or surplus in the market, ensuring stability. the demand curve (D) slopes downward, indicating that as price decreases, quantity demanded increases.The supply curve (S) slopes upward, showing that as price increases, quantity supplied rises.The intersection point (E) of both curves represents market equilibrium.The price at which demand of a good orservice is equal to its supply is equilibrium price 'P' and quantity is known as equilibrium quantity 'Q'.

28. Market disequilibrium-Excess demand

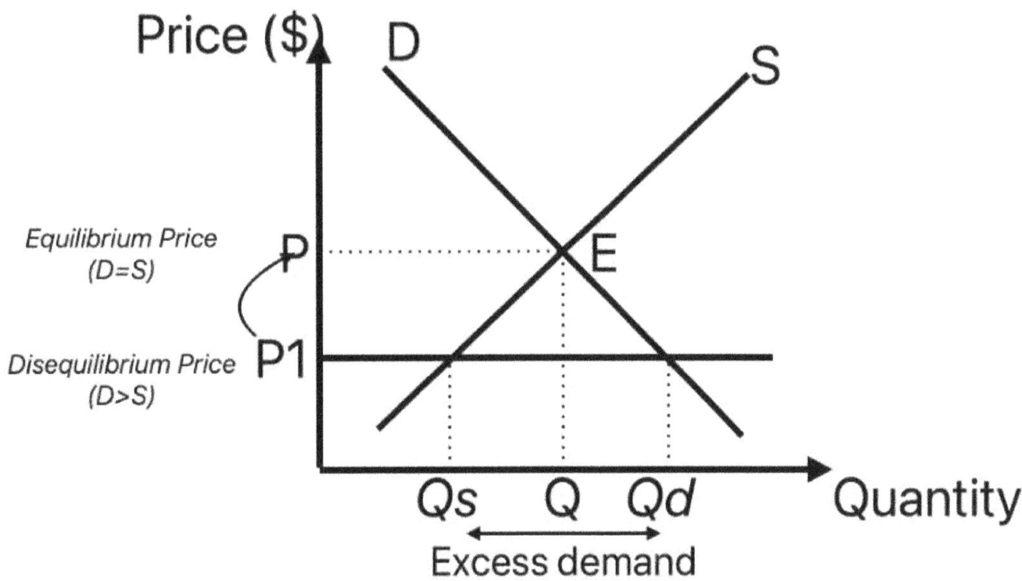

Fig 28: excess demand

Excess demand, also known as a shortage, occurs when the quantity demanded (QD) exceeds the quantity supplied (QS) at a given price. This happens when the market price is set below the equilibrium price, leading to more buyers willing to purchase the product than sellers willing to supply it. The demand curve (D) slopes downward, while the supply curve (S) slopes upward. Excess demand occurs when the price (30) is below the equilibrium price (50)At 30, quantity demanded (600) is greater than quantity supplied (200), creating a shortage. Consumers compete for the limited supply, pushing prices up. As prices rise, quantity suppliedincreases (producers supply more), and quantity demanded decreases (some consumers drop out).Eventually, the market moves back to equilibrium (E) where QD = QS.

29. Market disequilibrium-Excess supply

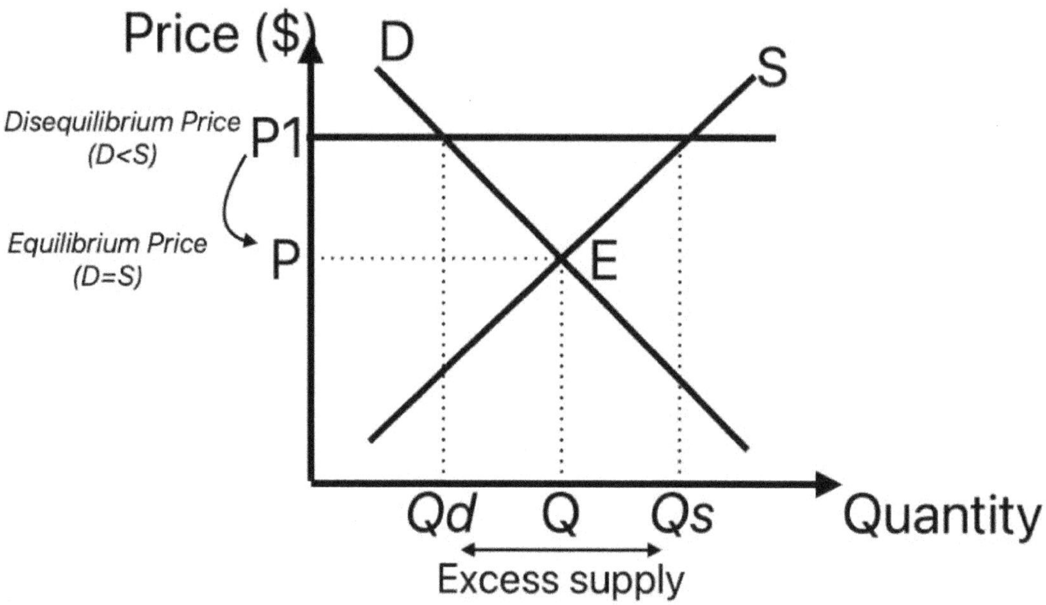

Fig 29: excess supply

Excess supply, also known as a surplus, occurs when the quantity supplied (Qs) exceeds he quantity demanded (Qd)at a given price. This happens when the market price is set above the equilibrium price, leadingto more goods available than consumers are willing to buy. The demand curve (D) slopes downward, while the supply curve (S) slopes upward. Excess supply occurs when the price (P1) is above the equilibrium price (P).At P1, quantity supplied (Qs) is greater than quantity demanded (Qd), creating a surplus. Market Reaction to Excess Supply: Producers lower prices to sell off excess stock. As prices decrease, quantity demanded increases (consumers buy more), and quantity supplied decreases(producers reduceoutput).Eventually, the market moves back to equilibrium (E) where QD = QS at price 'P'

30. Impact on equilibrium price if demand increases

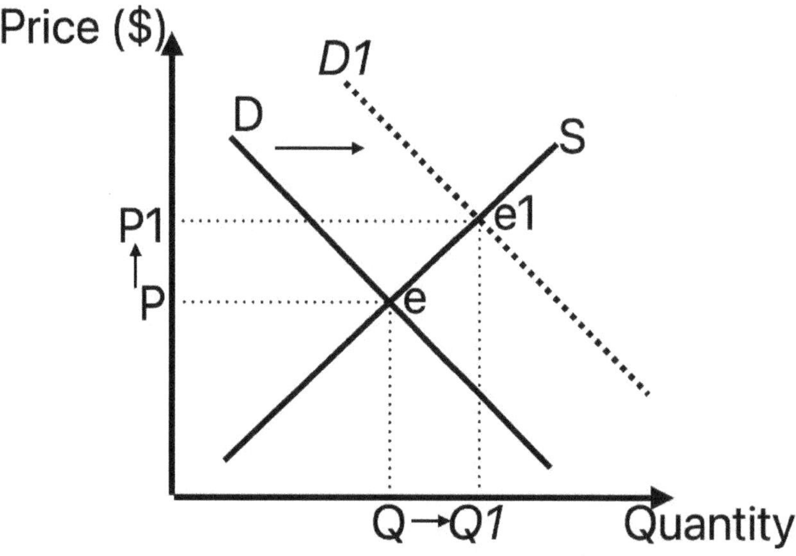

Fig 30: Impact on equilibrium price if demand increases

When demand increases, the demand curve shifts to the right from 'D' to 'D1', leading to a higher equilibrium price and quantity in the market. The original equilibrium is at 'e' (D=S) at 'P' and 'Q'. When demand increases, the demand curve shifts from D to D1. New equilibrium moves to e1, where the price increases to P1 and equilibrium quantity increases to 'Q1'

31. Impact on market price if demand decreases

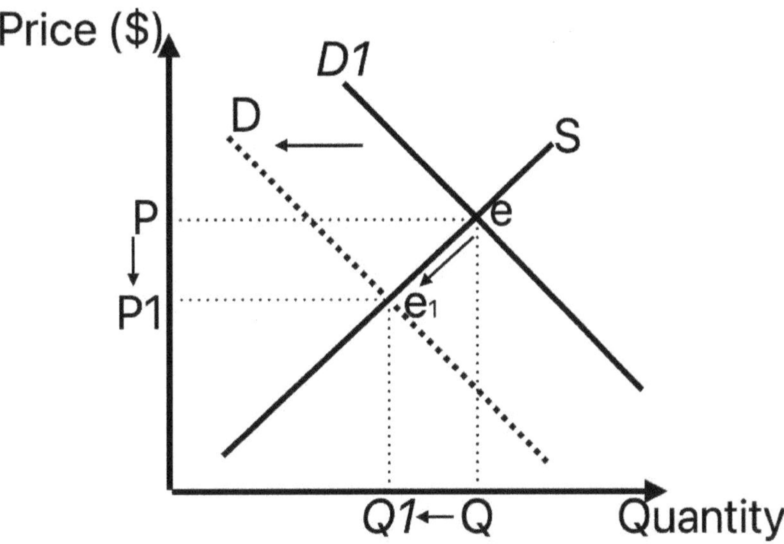

Fig 31:Impact on market price if demand decreases

When demand decreases, the demand curve shifts to the left from 'D1' to 'D',The equilibrium moves down from 'e' to 'e1'. The equilibrium price in the market decreases from P to P1 and equilibrium quantity decreases from 'Q' to 'Q1'

32. Impact on equilibrium price if supply increases

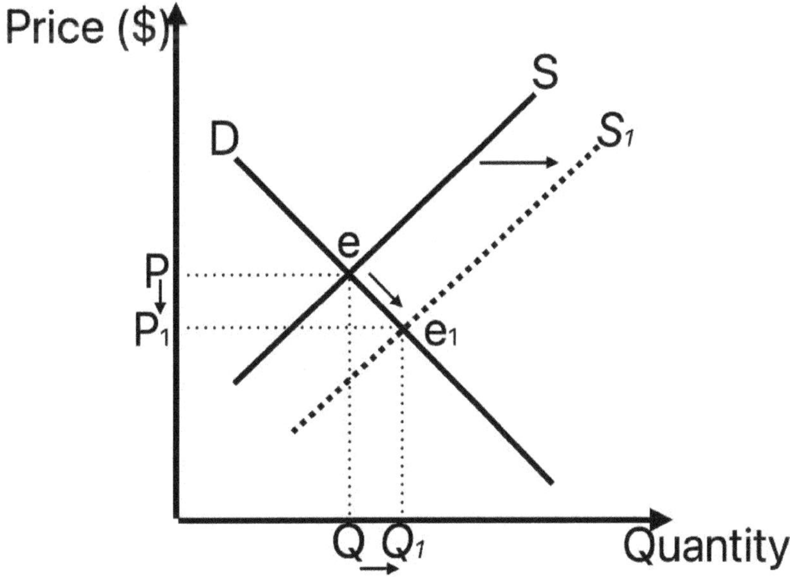

Fig 32:Impact on equilibrium price if supply increases

When supply increases, the supply curve shifts to the right FROM 'S' to 'S1', leading to a lower equilibrium price from 'P' to 'P1' and a higher equilibrium quantity in the market from 'Q' to 'Q1'

33. Impact on market price if supply decreases

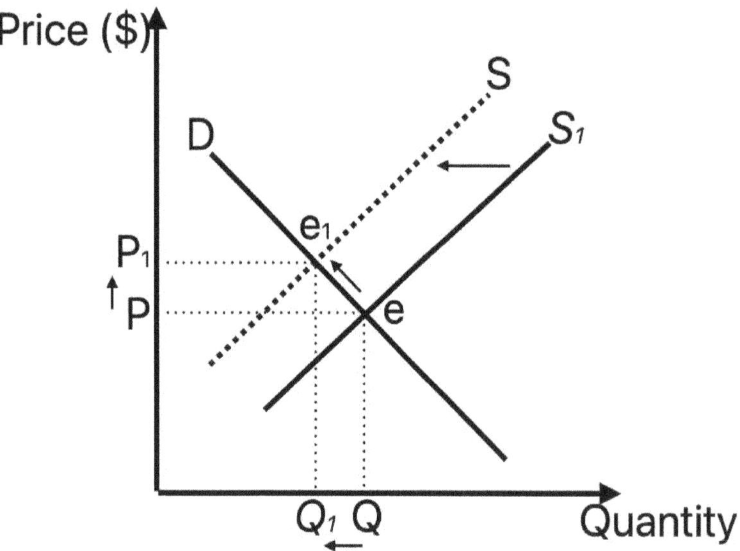

Fig 33:Impact on market price if supply decreases

When supply decreases, the supply curve shifts to the right from 'S1' to 'S', leading to a higher equilibrium price from 'P' to 'P1' and a lower equilibrium quantity in the market from 'Q' to 'Q1'

34. Maximum Price or Price Ceiling

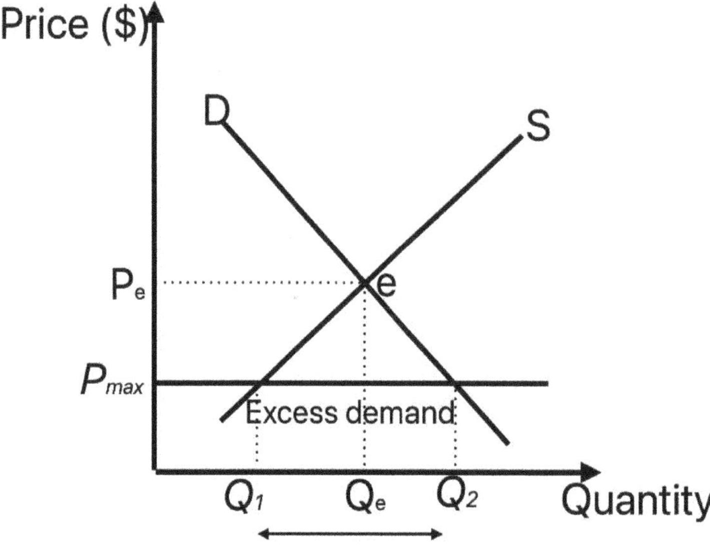

Fig 34: Maximum Price or Price Ceiling

A maximum price, also known as a price ceiling, is a government-imposed limit on how high a price can becharged for a good or service. It is set below the market equilibrium price to make essential goods and services more affordable for consumers. The initial equilibrium is at E (Pe, Qe). The government sets a priceceiling at Pmax, which is below the equilibrium price Pe.At Pc, demand (Q2) increases because prices are lower, but supply (Q1) decreases because producers are less willing to sell at that price. This results inexcess demand (shortage), shown as the gap between Q1 and Q2.

35. Minimum Price or Floor Price

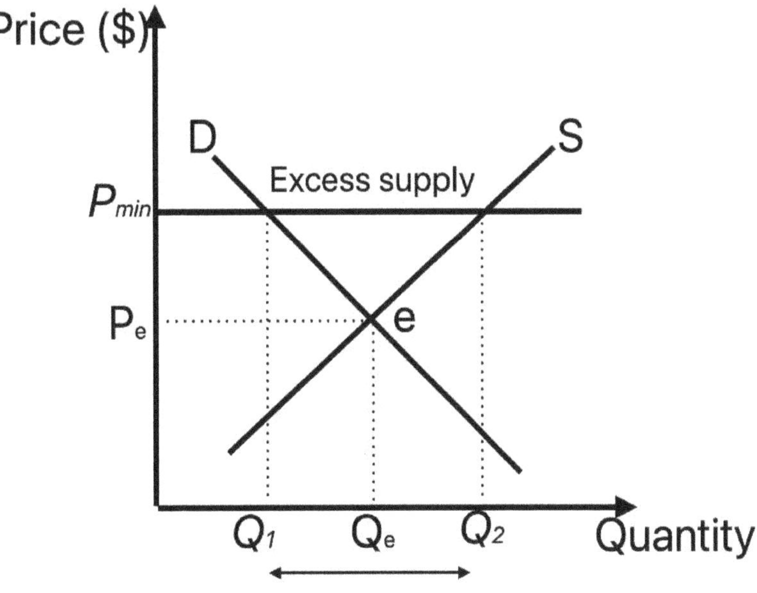

Fig 35: Minimum price

A minimum price, also known as a price floor, is a government-imposed lower limit on how much a good or service can be sold for. It is set above the market equilibrium price to ensure fair earnings for producers orworkers.The initial equilibrium is at E (Pe, Qe).The government sets a price floor at Pmin, which is above the equilibrium price Pe.At Pmin, supply (Q2) increases because producers can charge more, but demand (Q1) decreases because consumers are less willing to buy at higher prices. This results in excess supply (surplus), shown as the gap between Q1 and Q2.

36. Impact of indirect tax on market price

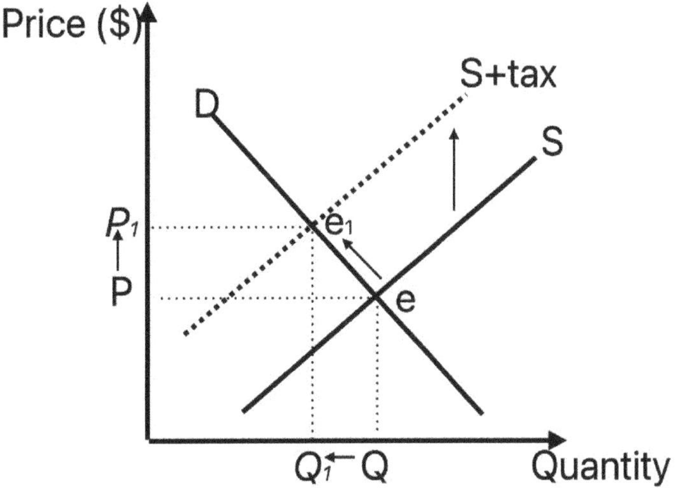

Fig 36: Impact of indirect tax on market price

An indirect tax is a tax imposed on goods and services rather than directly on income or profits. Examples include sales tax, excise duty, VAT (Value-Added Tax), and GST (Goods and Services Tax). When an indirect tax is levied, it affects market prices by increasing the cost of production, leading to higher prices for consumers and lower revenue for producers.After the tax is imposed, the supply curve shifts leftward.

37. Impact of subsidy on market price

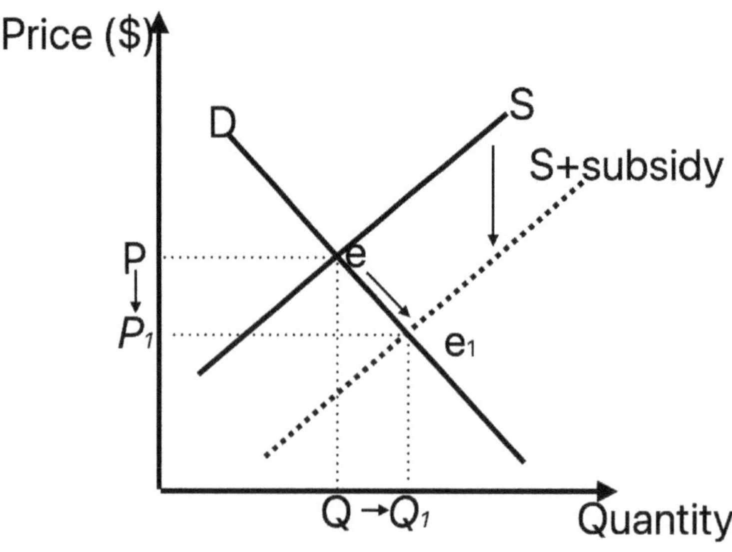

Fig 37: Impact of subsidy on market price

A subsidy is a financial assistance provided by the government to reduce the cost of production or encourage consumption of certain goods and services. When a subsidy is given to producers, it lowers their productioncosts, allowing them to supply more at a lower price, which benefits consumers. After the subsidy is provided,the supply curve shifts rightward from S to S+subsidy because producers can supply more at lower costs. Thisresults in a new equilibrium at E1, where the price decreases to P1, and the quantity increases to Q1.The government bears the cost of the subsidy per unit, which is the difference between the price received byproducers and the lower price paid by consumers.

38. Wage rate in labour market

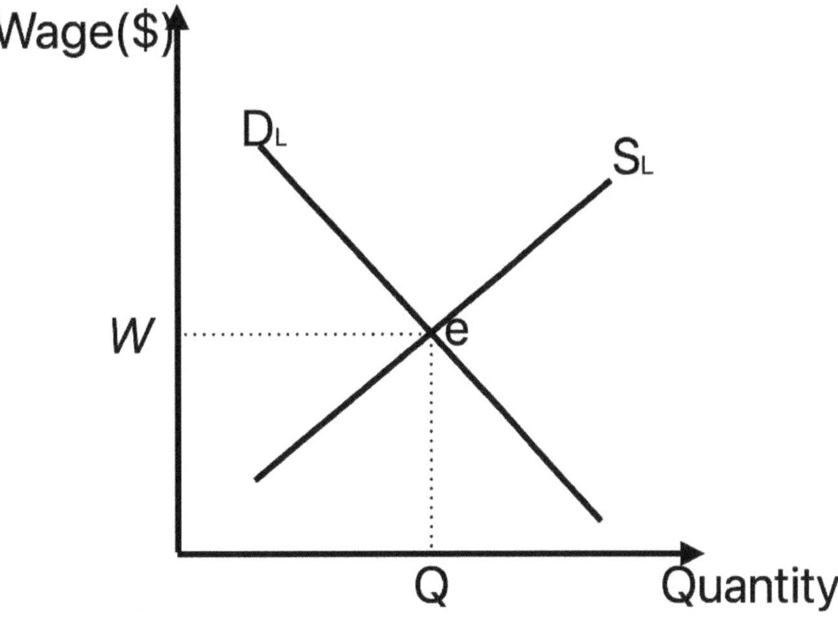

Fig 38: Wage rate

The **wage rate** is the price of labor in the market, determined by the forces of **demand (DL) and supply(SL)** of labor. It represents the payment workers receive for their services, typically expressed per hour, day, or month.The initial equilibrium is at 'e', where the wage rate is W and the quantity of labor employed is Q.

39. Minimum wages

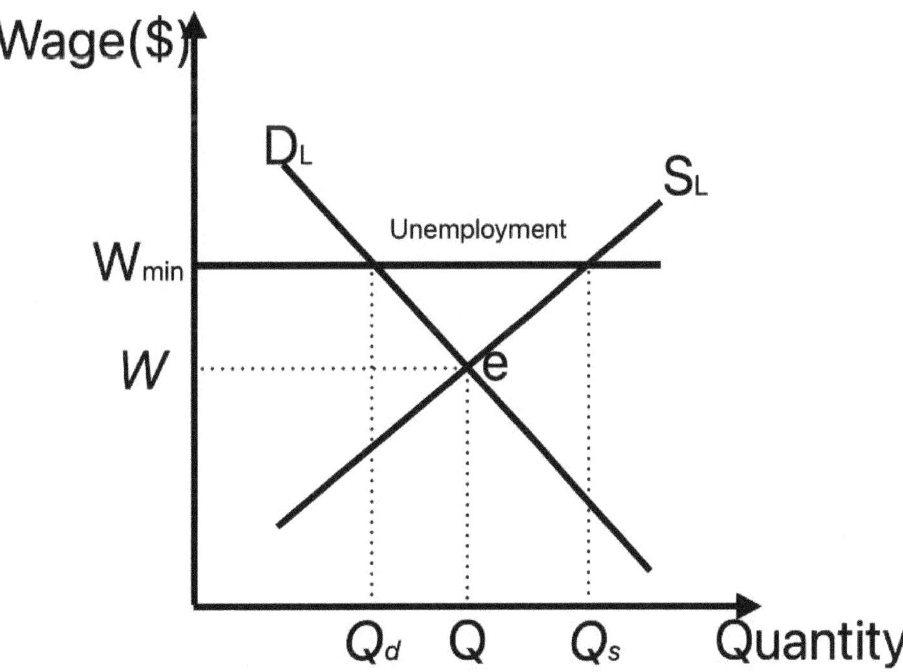

Fig 39: minimum wages

A minimum wage is the lowest legal wage that employers must pay their workers, set by the government to protect employees from exploitation and ensure a basic standard of living Without a minimum wage, the equilibrium wage is free market wage.When a minimum wage (Wmin) is set above the equilibriumwage , it creates excess supply (quantity of labour demanded is less than quantity of labour supplied) it creates unemployment because more workers are willing to work at higher wages,but firms hire fewer workers.

40. Impact of increase in demand for labour in the labor market

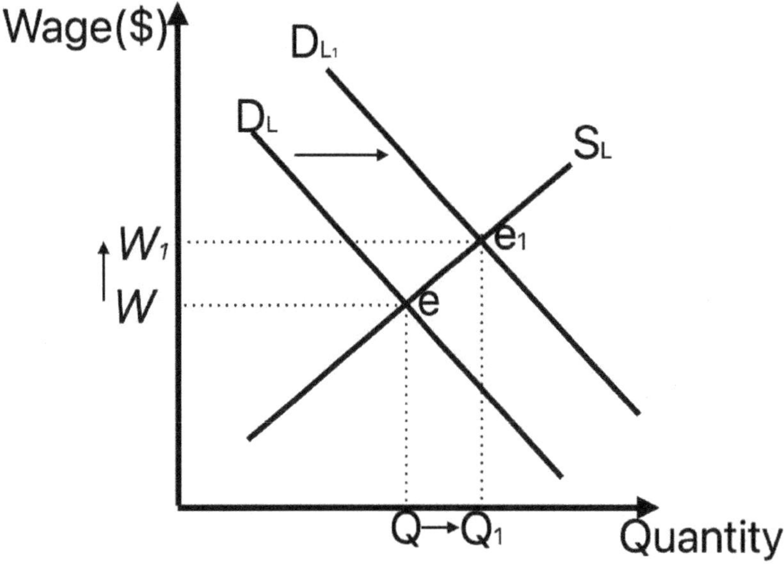

Fig 40: Impact of increase in demand for labour in the labor market

When the demand for labor increases, it means that employers are willing to hire more workers at any givenwage rate. This could be due to economic growth, technological advancements, increased business profitability, or a rise in demand for goods and services. The initial equilibrium is at 'e', with wage rate W and employment level Q.When demand for labor increases (DL → DL1), the new equilibrium moves to E1, where the wage rate rises to W1, and employment increases to Q1.

41. Impact of decrease in demand for labour in the labor market

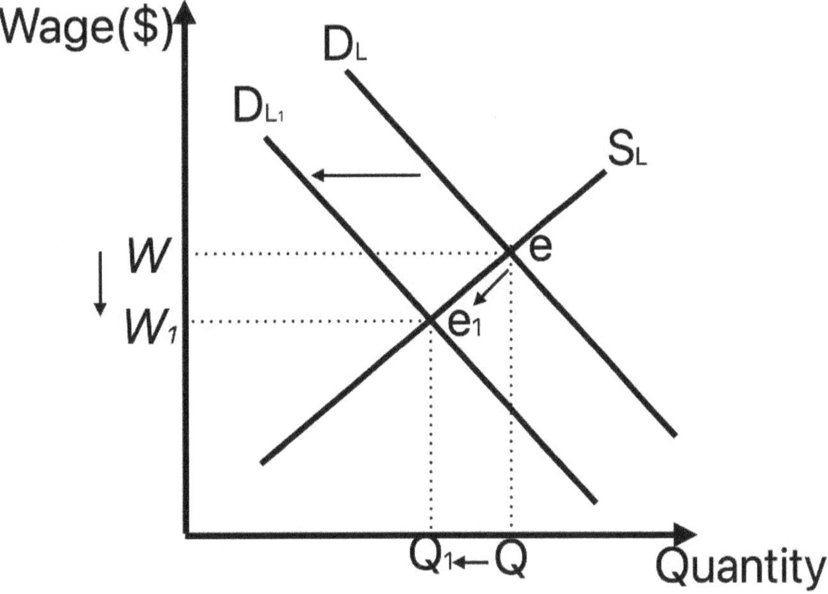

Fig 41: Impact of increase in demand for labour in the labor market

When the demand for labor decreases, it means employers require fewer workers at any given wage rate. This canhappen due to economic downturns, automation, reduced demand for goods and services, or outsourcing. The initial equilibrium is at 'e', with wage rate W and employment level Q. When demand for labor decreases (DL → DL1), the new equilibrium moves to 'e1', where the wage rate falls to W1, and employment decreases to Q1.

42. Impact of increase in supply of labour in the labor market

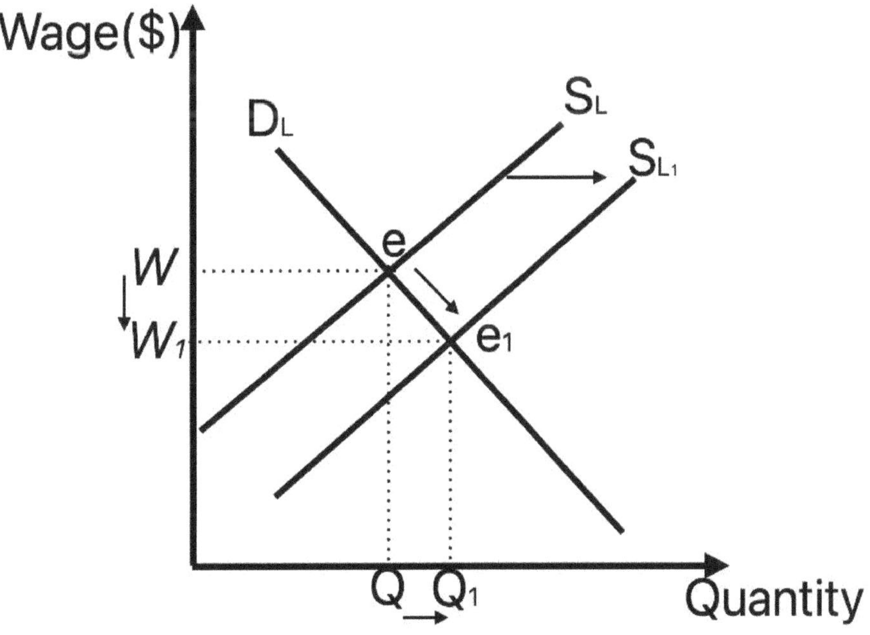

Fig 42: mpact of increase in supply of labour in the labor market

When the supply of labor increases, it means more workers are available for employment at every wage level. This can happen due to population growth, immigration, improved education, or changes in workforce participation (e.g., more women or retirees entering the labor market).The initial equilibrium is at 'e', with wage rate W and employment level Q.When labor supply increases (SL→ SL1), the new equilibrium moves to 'e1', where the wage rate falls to W1, and employment increases to Q1.

43. Impact of decrease in supply of labour in the labor market

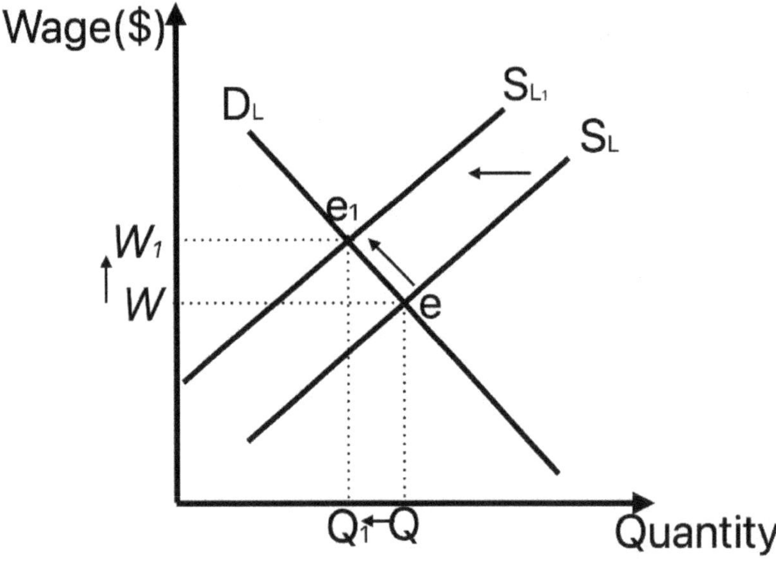

Fig 43: Impact of decrease in supply of labour in the labor market

When the supply of labor decreases, it means fewer workers are available for employment at every wage level. This can occur due to declining birth rates, emigration, aging populations, restrictive labor policies, or adecrease in workforce participation. The initial equilibrium is at 'e', with wage rate W and employment level Q. When labor supply decreases (SL → SL1), the new equilibrium moves to 'e1', where the wage rate rises to W1,and employment decreases to Q1.

44. Average fixed cost [AFC=TFC/Q]

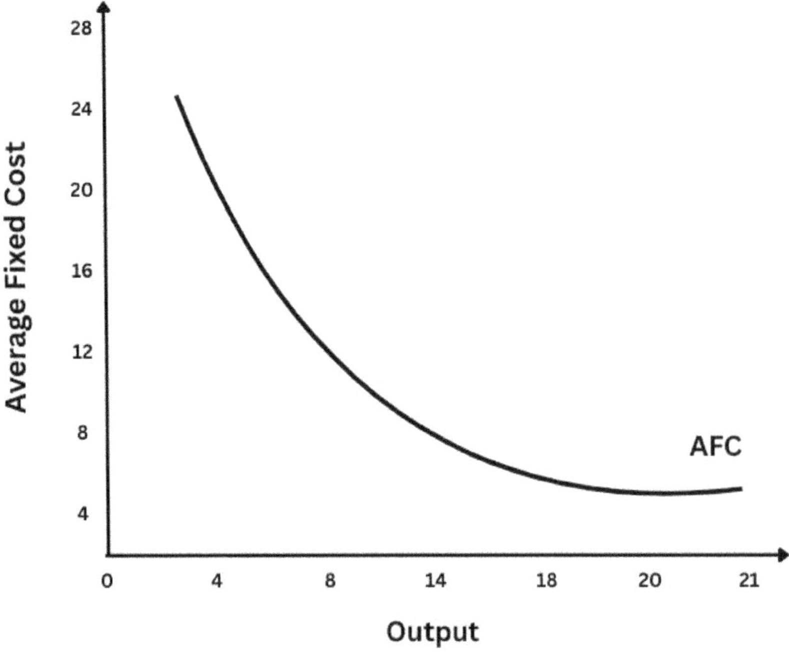

Enter CapFig 44: Average fixed cost

Average Fixed Cost (AFC) refers to the fixed cost per unit of output. It is calculated by dividing Total Fixed Cost (TFC)by the Quantity of Output (Q): AFC=TFC/Q. Always Decreasing – As output increases, AFCcontinuously declines because the fixed cost is spread over more units. Never Zero – AFC gets smaller but never reaches zero since TFC is always positive. Downward-Sloping Curve – AFC follows a rectangular hyperbola shape, meaning it falls steeply at low output levels and flattens at higher output levels.

45. Average Cost [AC=TC/Q]

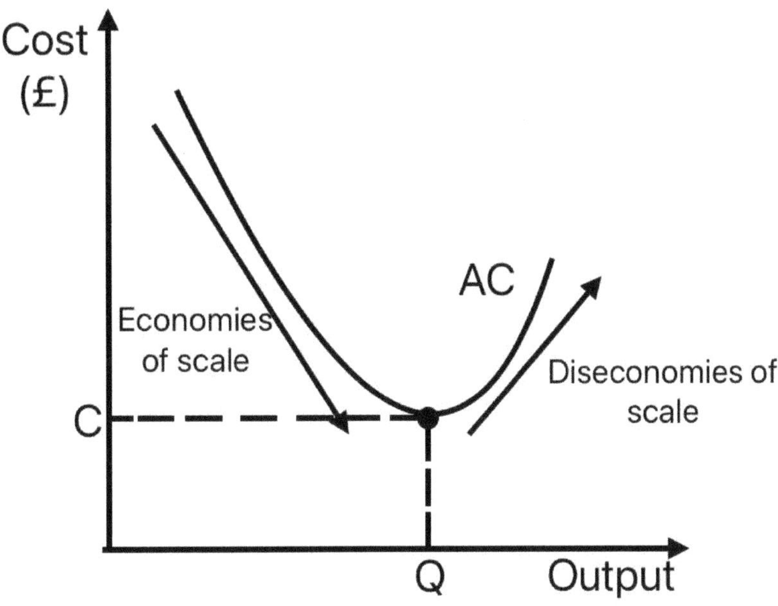

Fig 45: Average Cost

The Average Cost curve is U-shaped due to the initial decrease in costs (economies of scale) followed by an increase (diseconomies of scale).

46. Total Cost [TC=TVC+TFC]

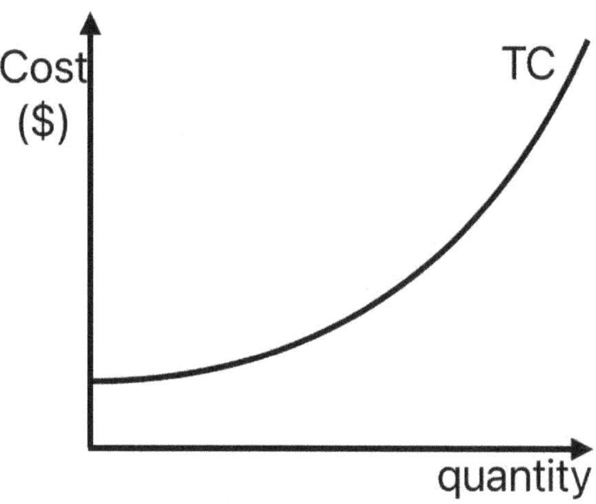

Fig 46: Total cost curve

Total Cost (TC) refers to the overall cost incurred by a firm in the production of goods or services. It is the sum of Total Fixed Cost (TFC) and Total Variable Cost (TVC).The TC curve starts from the level of TFC becausewhen output is zero, total cost equals fixed cost. As output increases, TC rises due to increasing TVC. Thecurve is upward-sloping and gets steeper at higher output levels due to diminishing returns.

47. Average variable cost [AVC=TVC/Q]

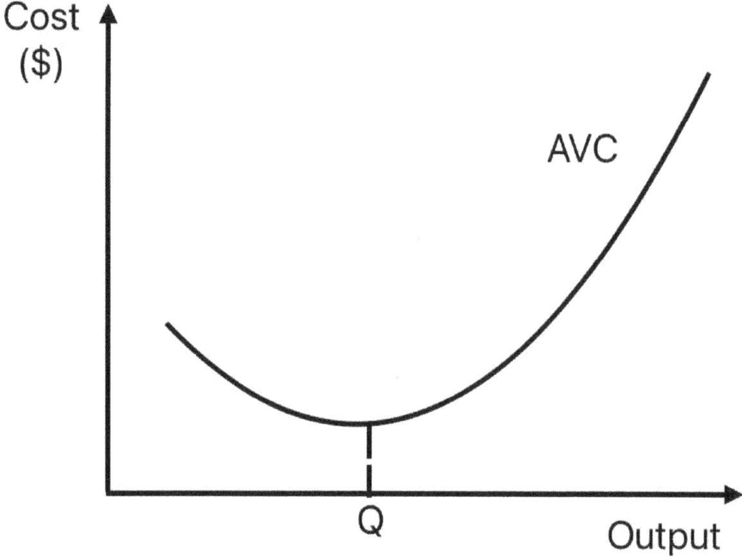

Fig 47: Average variable cost curve

Average Variable Cost (AVC) is the variable cost per unit of output. It is calculated by dividing Total Variable Cost (TVC) by the quantity of output (Q).U-Shaped Curve: Initially decreases due to increasing efficiency(economies of scale) but later rises due to diminishing marginal returns. Depends on TVC: As TVC increases, AVC also changes accordingly. Never touches the X-axis: AVC is never zero as long as production takes place.

48. Total Variable cost [TVC]

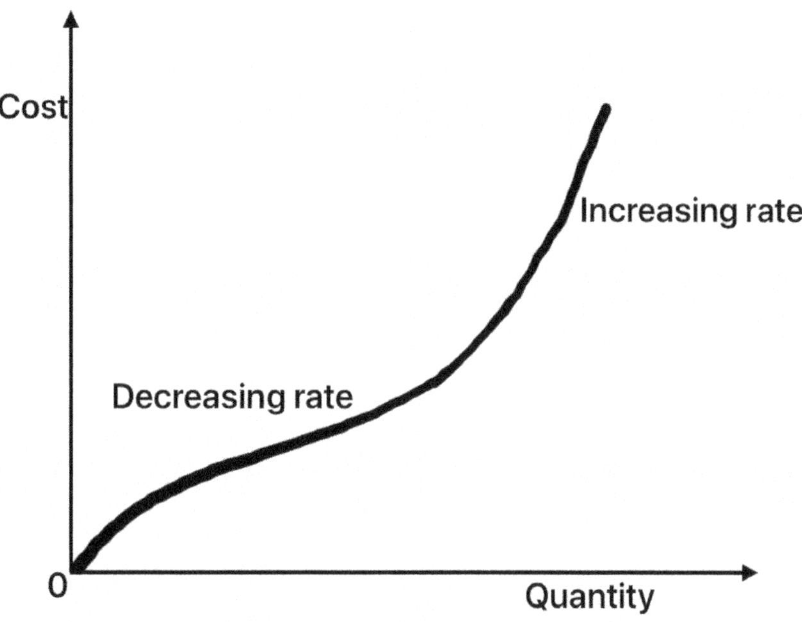

Fig 48: Total variable cost curve

Total Variable Cost (TVC) refers to the cost incurred on variable inputs, which change with the level of output. These costs rise as production increases and fall when production decreases. TVC is zero when output is zero(since no production takes place).TVC increases as output rises but at a changing rate: Initially, TVC rises at adecreasing rate (efficiency gains). Later, TVC rises at an increasing rate (diminishing marginal returns).

49. Progressive tax

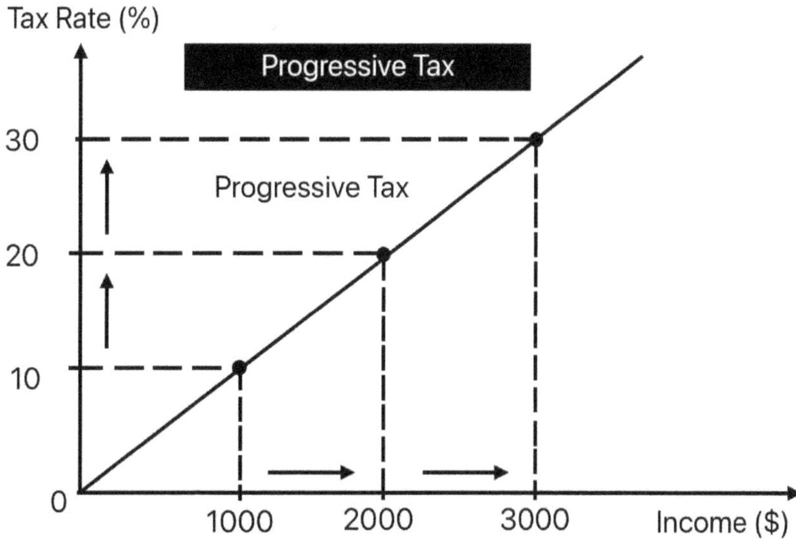

Fig 49: Progressive tax

A progressive tax is a taxation system where the tax rate increases as income increases. This means thatindividuals or businesses with higher incomes pay a higher percentage of their income in taxes compared tothose with lower incomes. In the above diagram as the income increases from 1000$ to 2000$ the tax rate increases from 10% to 20%

50. Regressive tax

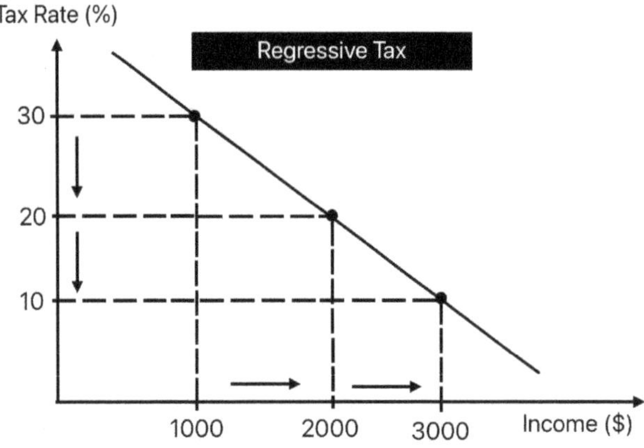

Fig 50: Regressive tax

A regressive tax is a tax system where the tax rate decreases as income increases. This means that lower-income individuals pay a higher proportion of their income in taxes compared to higher-income individuals. In the above diagram as the income increases from 1000$ to 2000$ the tax rate decreases from 30% to 20%

51. Proportional tax

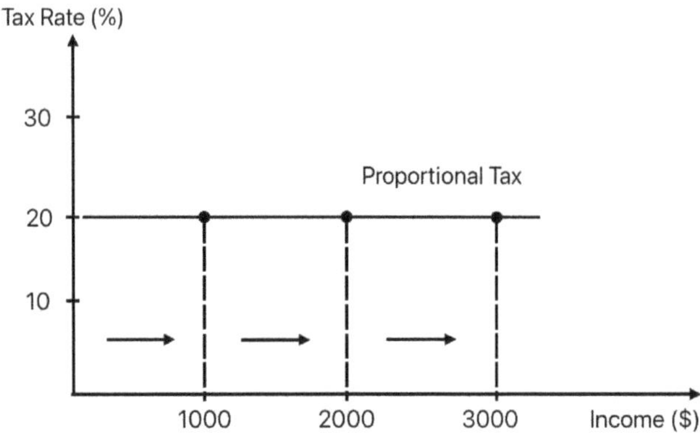

Fig 51: Proportional tax

A proportional tax, also known as a flat tax, is a tax system in which the tax rate remains the same for all income levels. This means that everyone pays the same percentage of their income in taxes, regardless of how much they earn. In the above diagram as the income increases from 1000$ to 2000$ the tax rate remains at 20%.

52. Short run economic growth in PPC

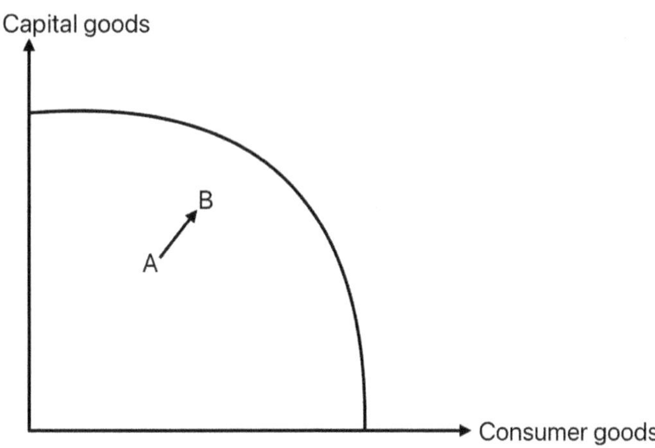

Fig 52: Short run economic growth

Short-run economic growth occurs when an economy increases its output of goods and services by utilizing its existing resources more efficiently. This is represented by a movement from a point inside the PPC 'A' to a point closer to or on the curve 'B' rather than an outward shift of the curve.

53. Long run economic growth in PPC

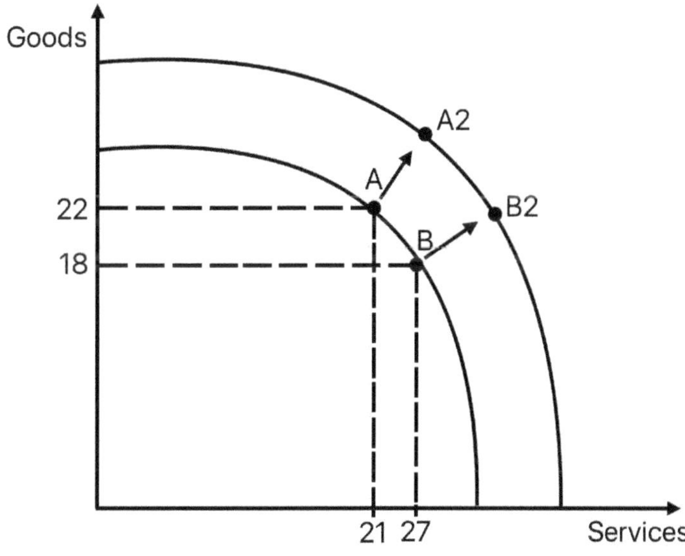

Fig 53: Long run economic frowth

Long-run economic growth refers to the increase in an economy's productive capacity over time, allowing to produce more goods and services. In the PPC model, this is represented by an outward shift of the curve, indicating that the economy can produce more of both goods due to improvements in resources or technology.

54. Demand pull inflation

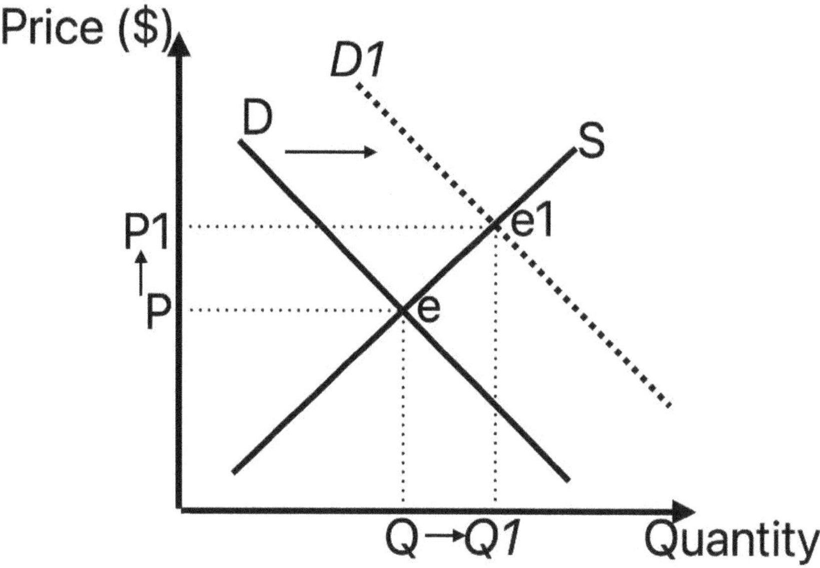

Fig 54: Demand pull inflation

In the Aggregate Demand & Aggregate Supply (AD-AS) framework, demand-pull inflation is shown by a rightward shift in the AD curve [D1 to D2], causing an increase in the price level P1TO P2.

55. Cost push inflation

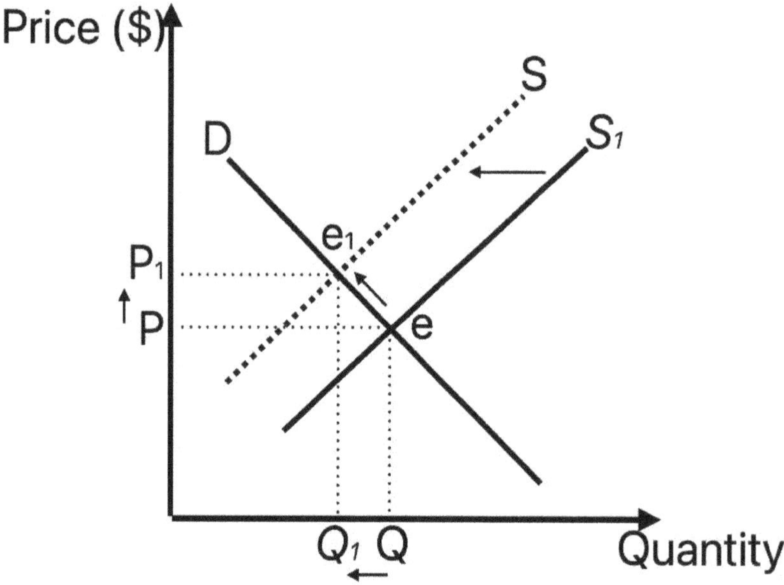

Fig 55: Cost push inflation

In the Aggregate Demand & Aggregate Supply (AD-AS) framework, cost push inflation is shown by a leftward shift in the AS curve [SRAS1 to SRAS2], causing an increase in the price level P1TO P2. [SRAS is short run aggregate supply].

56. Floating exchange rate

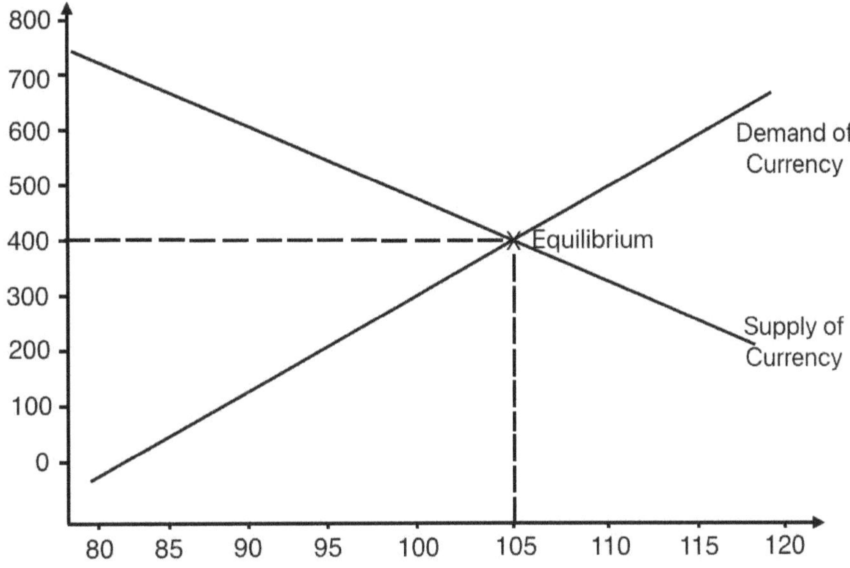

Fig 56: Floating exchange rate

A floating exchange rate is a currency system in which the value of a country's currency is determined by market forces—specifically, supply and demand in the foreign exchange (Forex) market—without direct government or central bank intervention. If the above diagram represents the foreign exchange market of Indian rupee (INR) in terms of Riyal. In the above diagram 400 is the exchange rate, meaning 400 INR will be required to buy one Riyal.

57. Impact of increasing imports on exchange rate

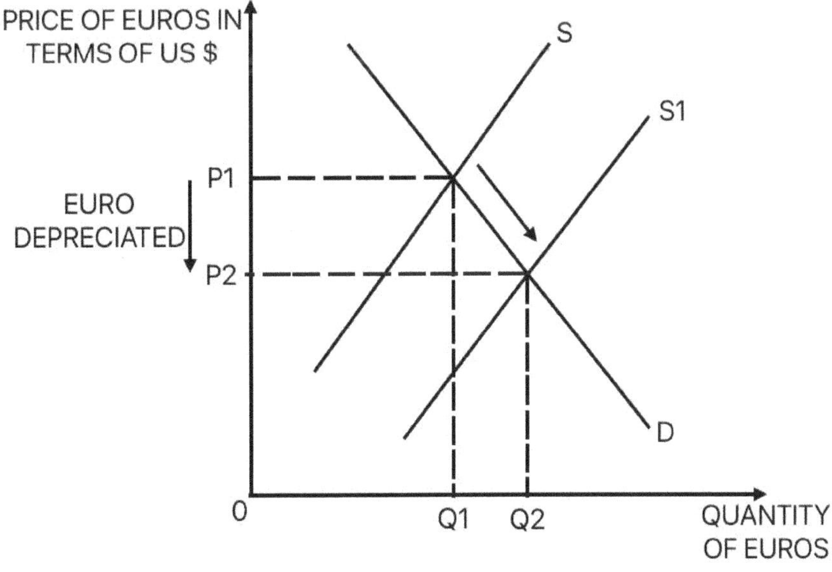

Fig 57: Impact of increasing imports on exchange rate

This graph illustrates the impact of increasing imports on the exchange rate. Due to higher imports from USA to germany, demand for $ will increase by germany. They will supply euros to buy $. The supply of euros will shift right S to S1. The rightward shift in the supply curve of euros lead to its depreciation in the exchange rate as the exchange rate falls from P1 to P2. That is less $ is required to buy euros.

58. Impact of increasing exports on exchange rate

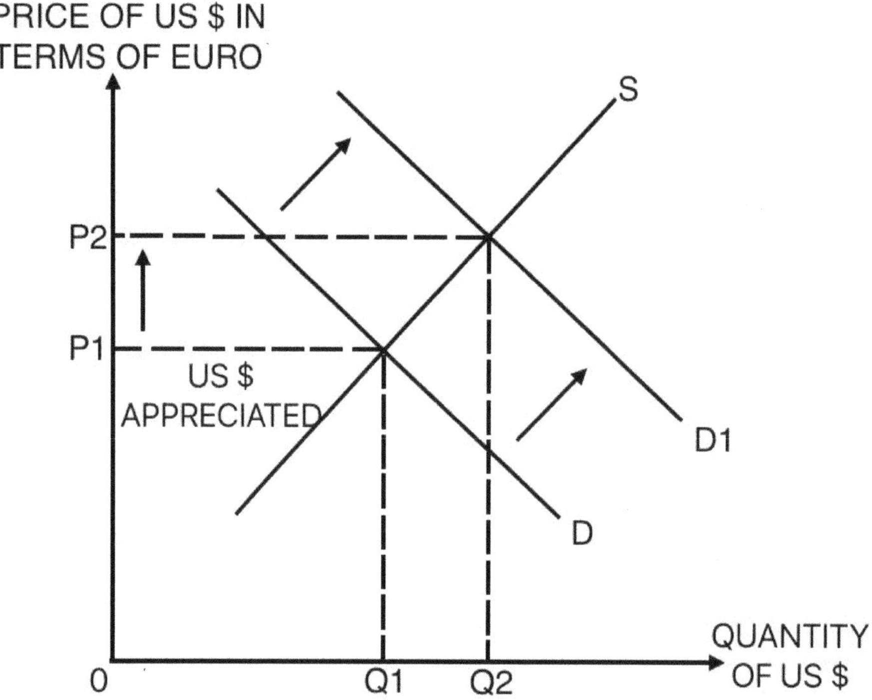

Fig 58: Impact of increasing exports on exchange rate

This graph illustrates the impact of increasing exports on the exchange rate. Due to higher exports by the united states to germany, demand for $ increaseed.The demand curve of $ shifts right [D to D1]. The exchange rate rises from P to P1. This is known as appreciation of $ in terms of Euro. More euro is required to buy $.

THREE

UNIT 1- THE BASIC ECONOMIC PROBLEM

LEARNING OBJECTIVES

LO1: Definition and examples of the economic problem in the contexts of: consumers; workers; producers; and governments. The difference between economic goods and free goods.

LO2: Definitions and examples of land, labour, capital and enterprise. Examples of the nature of each factor of production. The influences on the mobility of the various factors. The causes of changes in the quantity and quality of the various factors.

LO3: Definition and examples of opportunity cost in different contexts. Decisions made by consumers, workers, producers and governments when allocating their resources.

LO4: Definition, drawing and interpretation of appropriate diagrams. The significance of the location of productionpoints. Movements along a PPC and opportunity cost. The causes and consequences of shifts in a PPC in terms of an economy's growth

TERMS TO REMEMBER

1. **Economic Problem:** The fundamental issue of scarcity, where unlimited wants exceed limitedresources.
2. **Problem of Choice:** The need to make decisions on resource allocation due to scarcity.
3. **Economic Goods:** Goods that require scarce resources to produce and have an opportunity cost.
4. **Factors of Production:** The four essential inputs used in production—land, labor, capital, andenterprise.
5. **Free Goods:** Goods available in unlimited supply, such as air or sunlight, with no opportunity cost.
6. **Land:** Natural resources used in production, like minerals, water, and forests.
7. **Labour:** The human effort, both physical and mental, used in production.
8. **Capital:** Man-made resources (machinery, tools) used in production.
9. **Enterprise:** The ability to take risks and organize other factors of production to create goods and services.
10. **Mobility:** The ease with which resources or labour can move between different uses or locations.
11. **Geographical Mobility:** The ability of labour or resources to move between locations.
12. **Occupational Mobility:** The ability of labor to switch between different types of jobs.
13. **Opportunity Cost:** The next best alternative foregone when making a choice.
14. **PPC (Production Possibility Curve):** A graph showing maximum possible output combinations of two goods given limited resources.
15. **Allocation of Resources:** The way resources are distributed among different uses.

STRUCTURED QUESTIONS [2,4,6,8 marks]

1. Why does the basic economic problem arise? [2/4]

The **basic economic problem** arises due to the fundamental issue of **scarcity**—there are **limited resources** but **unlimited wants and needs**. Since resources such as land, labor, capital, and entrepreneurship are finite, societies must make choices about how to allocate them effectively.

For example, a government must decide whether to allocate more funds to **healthcare or education**. If it spends more on **hospitals**, there may be fewer resources left for building **schools**. Similarly, a car manufacturer like **Toyota** must decide whether to produce more **electric vehicles (EVs)** or **petrol cars** based on available resources. This necessity to choose how to use scarce resources efficiently is at the heart of the basic economic problem.

2. What are the basic economic problems?[6]

The basic economic problems revolve around the three key questions:

What to produce? Since resources are limited, economies must decide which goods and services to produce. For instance, should a country invest in military weapons or public transport? If a nation like South Korea prioritizes technology and electronics, it may become a leader in innovation, while a country focusing on agriculture may ensure food security.

How to produce? This question concerns the methods of production—should firms use labour- intensive or capital-intensive techniques? For example, in India, where labour is abundant, firms may preferhandmade textiles, while in Germany, industries rely on automation and robots due to higher wages.

For whom to produce? The distribution of goods and services must be decided. A market-driven economy like the USA relies on price mechanisms, where those who can afford goods get them. However, in a socialist economy like Cuba, the government ensures equal access to necessities such as healthcare and education.

3. Differentiate between the four factors of production based on occupational and geographical mobility.[8]

The four factors of production—land, labor, capital, and enterprise—differ in terms of their occupational mobility(ability to switch to different uses) and geographical mobility (ability to move from one location to another).

Land

Occupational Mobility: Land is highly immobile occupationally. A piece of land used for farming cannot easily be used for setting up a factory without significant investment and changes.

Geographical Mobility: Land is completely immobile geographically since it is fixed in one place and cannot be moved elsewhere.

Labor

Occupational Mobility: Labor has varied occupational mobility. Skilled workers with specialized knowledge (e.g., doctors, engineers) have low mobility, while unskilled workers (e.g., manual laborers) can switch jobs more easily.

Geographical Mobility: Labor is moderately mobile geographically. Workers can move to different locations for jobs, but factors like family, cultural differences, and legal restrictions can limit their movement.

Capital

Occupational Mobility: Capital has high occupational mobility, as machines, tools, and money can be repurposed for different industries. For example, a truck used for construction can also be used for transportation services.

Geographical Mobility: Capital is relatively mobile geographically. Financial capital (money) is highly mobile, but physical capital (machinery, factories) may face transportation and relocation challenges.

Enterprise

Occupational Mobility: Enterprise has high occupational mobility because entrepreneurs can shift from one business sector to another if they have the required skills and resources.

Geographical Mobility: Enterprise is highly mobile as entrepreneurs can set up businesses in different locations, though legal and cultural barriers may sometimes restrict movement.

Thus, among the four factors, land is the least mobile, while enterprise is the most mobile in both occupational and geographical terms.

4. State one cause of changes in the quantity and quality of the four factors of production.[4]

The **quantity and quality** of the factors of production can change due to various reasons.

Land – Natural disasters or climate change can reduce the quality of land. For example, rising desertification in Africa has decreased agricultural productivity.

Labor – Education and training can improve the quality of labor. For example, Germany's vocational trainingsystemenhances the skill level of workers.

Capital – Technological advancements can improve capital. For instance, the development of AI- powered machineryhas made production more efficient in factories.

Entrepreneurship – Government policies such as startup grants can increase the number of entrepreneurs. For example, Singapore'sbusiness-friendly environmentencourages more startups.

5. Explain two causes and two consequences of rightward shifts in a PPC.[6]

A **rightward shift in the Production Possibility Curve (PPC)** indicates economic growth, meaning that an economy can produce **more goods and services** than before.

Causes of a Rightward Shift in PPC:

Technological Advancements: Innovations in technology improveproductivity, allowing more goods to be produced with the same resources. Example: **Automation in car manufacturing**, such as the use of **robotic**

arms in Tesla factories, increases efficiency and output.

Increase in Factors of Production: If a country has more resources (land, labor, capital, and entrepreneurship), its PPC expands. Example: **China's large labor force** and infrastructure investments have significantly boosted its production capacity over the last few decades.

Consequences of a Rightward Shift in PPC:

Higher Economic Growth and Living Standards: As more goods and services are produced, the economy grows, leading to higher income and better quality of life.Example: **South Korea's transformation** from a developing to a high-income country was driven by industrialization and innovation in technology.

Lower Unemployment: A growing economy requires more workers, reducing unemployment levels. Example: When **Apple expands its factories**, it creates thousands of jobs in **China and the USA**, improving employment rates.

The **basic economic problem** arises due to **scarcity** and the need for efficient resource allocation. Thefour factors of production play a crucial role in determining an economy's capacity, and their mobility affects economic efficiency. **Changes in these factors** influence production possibilities, leading toeconomic growth or decline. By understanding the causes and consequences of shifts in production capacity, economies can **implement policies to ensure sustainable growth and improved living standards**.

CASE STUDY:The Basic Economic Problem in India

India, home to over **1.4 billion people**, faces the **fundamental economic problem of scarcity**, where**unlimited wants must be met with limited resources**. This issue is evident across different sectors of the economy. **Consumers** in India, especially those in the middle and lower-income groups, must decide how to allocate their income between essential goods like food and housing and discretionary expenses like electronics and entertainment. For instance, India's **per capita income in 2023 stood at approximately $2,610**, but income inequality means purchasing power varies significantly across different regions and social groups.

For **workers**, trade-offs exist in employment choices. India's **unemployment rate was 7.6% in 2023**, but many people are engaged in informal jobs with **low wages and job insecurity**. Workers must decide between stable government jobs (such as banking or civil services) and private-sector jobs, which may offerhigher salaries but come with **less job security**. In the **producer sector**, businesses like Tata Motors must decide whether to invest in electric vehicle production (given rising demand and government incentives) or focus on improving conventional fuel efficiency. At the **government level**, policymakers must make crucial spending decisions. In the **Union Budget 2023-24**, India allocated ₹**10 lakh crore ($122 billion) to infrastructure**, while healthcare spending was ₹**89,155 crore ($11 billion)**. These decisions reflect the government's challenge of balancing long-term growth with immediate needs.

In this context, distinguishing between **economic goods and free goods** is essential. **Economic goods**, suchas electricity, petroleum, and housing, are scarce and have an **opportunity cost**. On the other hand,**free goods** like air and sunlight do not carry an opportunity cost. However, with increasing pollution, evenair quality has deteriorated, making clean air an **economic good** in many Indian cities. For example, Delhi's **Air Quality Index (AQI) regularly exceeds 400**, forcing the government to invest in air purifiers and pollution control measures.

Capacity of production

India has 3.28 million square kilometers of land, with vast natural resources like coal (India ranks 2nd in production globally), fertile agricultural land, and a long coastline that supports trade. However, issues likeland degradation, deforestation, and urbanization reduce the availability of productive land. India has a labor force of over 500 million people, but labor productivity remains lower than in developed economies. The government's Skill India initiative aims to improve workforce skills, yet challenges persist, such as the mismatch between education and industry requirements.

Capital investment has surged, with foreign direct investment (FDI) inflows reaching $71 billion in 2022-23. Industries such as IT, pharmaceuticals, and renewable energy have seen significant capital growth, reflecting economic modernization. Entrepreneurs like Mukesh Ambani (Reliance), Narayana Murthy (Infosys), and Ritesh

Agarwal (OYO) have driven India's corporate growth. The startup ecosystem is thriving, with India now having over100 unicorn startups (valued over $1 billion), largely in technology and e-commerce sectors. Changes in thequantity and quality of these factors occur due to various reasons. For example, India's working-age population isprojected to peak at 65% by 2036, but without proper education and employment opportunities, this demographic advantage may not be fully realized. Government initiatives like "Make in India" and "Digital India" aim to improve factor efficiency and utilization.

Decision-Making

In 2022, India's average monthly household income was around ₹23,000 ($280), and consumers must prioritize necessities over luxuries. A family may choose between buying a car or saving for a child's education.

Many Indian students face the choice of pursuing higher education (which delays earnings but improves long-term income prospects) or entering the job market early. For example, an engineering graduate might take an IT job in Bangalore instead of pursuing further studies. Companies like Tata and Mahindra must decide between investing in electric vehicles (aligned with global trends) or improving petrol/diesel car efficiency. During the COVID-19 pandemic, the Indian government reallocated ₹35,000 crore ($4.3 billion) towards vaccine procurement, which meant delaying certain infrastructure projects. These decisions illustrate how scarcity forces trade-offs across various levels of the economy.

Economic Growth in India

India's Production Possibility Curve (PPC) reflects economic efficiency, trade-offs, and growth potential. If resources are underutilized due to unemployment (7.6%) or inefficiencies, production falls inside the PPC. A movement alongthe PPC occurs when India reallocates resources—e.g., shifting investment from agriculture (17% of GDP) to services(53% of GDP). India's economic growth, driven by increased labour productivity, infrastructure investments, and technology advancements. India's GDP grew by 7.2% in 2022-23, largely due to industrial and technological expansion. Conversely, a negative shock such as climate change, resource depletion, or economic downturns (like the slowdown during the pandemic) can shift the PPC inward.

Answer the following questions:

1 Mark Questions

Q1. What is the fundamental economic problem India faces?

A1. The fundamental economic problem India faces is **scarcity**, where unlimited wants must be met with limited resources.

Q2. Give an example of an economic good mentioned in the case study.

A2. An example of an economic good mentioned in the case study is **electricity** (or petroleum/housing).

2 Marks Questions:

Q3. Define opportunity cost and provide an example from the case study.

A3. Opportunity cost is the next best alternative foregone when making a decision. An example from the case study

is the Indian government reallocating ₹35,000 crore ($4.3 billion) towards vaccine procurement, which meant delaying certain infrastructure projects.

Q4. Explain why clean air is considered an economic good in many Indian cities.

A4. Clean air is considered an economic good in many Indian cities because it is scarce due to pollution and has anopportunity cost. The government must invest in air purifiers and pollution control measures, making it no longer freely available like a true free good.

3 Marks Questions:

Q5. Identify and explain two factors affecting the production capacity of India.

A5. Two factors affecting the production capacity of India

Natural Resources: India has vast coal reserves and fertile land, but land degradation and deforestation reduce productive land availability.

Labor Force: India has over 500 million workers, but low labor productivity and a skills gap hinder efficiency despite initiatives like Skill India.

4 Marks Question:

Q6. Explain how India's economic growth is reflected in its production possibility curve (PPC).

PPC Representation – The Production Possibility Curve (PPC) shows the maximum output an economy can produce with available resources.

Economic Growth – India's 7.2% GDP growth in 2022-23 reflects an outward shift in the PPC due to higher productivity, infrastructure investments, and technological advancements.

Sectoral Shifts – A movement along the PPC occurs as resources shift from agriculture (17% of GDP) to services (53% of GDP), reflecting India's transition towards a more service-based economy.

Negative Shocks – Factors like climate change, resource depletion, or a financial crisis can shift the PPC inward, reducing India's economic capacity.

6 Marks Question:

Q7. Analyse how scarcity affects decision-making at different levels of the Indian economy. A7. Scarcity forces individuals, businesses, and the government to make choices:

Consumers – With an average household income of ₹23,000 ($280), Indian families must prioritize necessities like food and housing over luxuries like cars or entertainment.

Businesses – Companies like Tata Motors must decide between investing in electric vehicles (aligning with trends and incentives) or improving fuel efficiency in petrol/diesel cars.

Government – Policymakers must allocate budgets efficiently, such as choosing to invest ₹10 lakh crore ($122 billion) in infrastructure while only ₹89,155 crore ($11 billion) went to healthcare in 2023-24

CASE STUDY: Economic Problems in Colombia

Colombia, a country with a population of over 52 million, faces the fundamental economic problem of scarcity. Withlimited resources and unlimited wants, decisions must be made at the consumer, producer, and government levels. The challenge is balancing economic growth, resource allocation, and sustainability while addressing socialinequalities. Consumers in Colombia must decide how to allocate their income between essential needs anddiscretionary spending. The income inequality gap in Colombia is one of the highest in Latin America, with a Gini coefficient of 0.54 in 2023. Colombian businesses must **allocate resources** efficiently. Key sectors like **oil, coffee, and manufacturing** must decide where to invest

The Colombian government must distribute resources among healthcare, education, infrastructure, and defense.

Colombia's economic growth depends on how resources are allocated between industries. Economic growth is driven by investment and infrastructure. Climate change and political instability can shift the PPC inward, limiting production capacan be a deterring factor to the real GDP of the country.

Answer the following questions

1 Mark Questions

Q1. What is meant by scarcity?

A: Scarcity refers to the limited availability of resources to meet unlimited human wants.

Q2. Define opportunity cost.

A: Opportunity cost is the next best alternative forgone when a choice is made.

Q3. Name one economic sector that employs the highest percentage of Colombians.

A: Services sector (55%).

2 Mark Questions

Q4. Explain why informal employment a challenge in Colombia.

A: Informal employment provides **low wages** and **job insecurity**. Workers lack **benefits** like health insurance and pensions, making their financial situation unstable.

Q5. What trade-off does the Colombian government face in allocating its budget?

A: The government must balance spending on infrastructure, healthcare, education, and defense. Investing more in one sector (e.g., **infrastructure**) means reducing funds for another (e.g., social welfare**).

3 Mark Questions

Q6. Explain how an increase in foreign investment can shift Colombia's PPC outward.

Foreign investment increases capital resources and technology, boosting productivity. It leads to industrial expansion, increasing output capacity. More efficient resource use allows Colombia to produce more goods and services, shifting the PPC outward.

Q8. How does climate change affect Colombia's economic growth? Floods and droughts reduce agricultural output, shifting the PPC inward. Damaged infrastructure leads to higher government repair costs.

Reduced tourism and exports slow economic growth.

4 Mark Questions

Q9. Explain two factors that determine consumer spending patterns in Colombia.

Income Levels: Low-income groups spend more on necessities (food, housing). High-income groups have more disposable income for discretionary spending.

Inflation and Prices: Rising prices reduce purchasing power, limiting luxury spending. High inflation makes saving difficult, forcing people to spend more on essentials.

Q10. How does opportunity cost apply to Colombia's automobile industry?

Car manufacturers like Renault and GM must decide whether to invest in electric vehicles (EVs) or improve fuelefficiency in petrol cars.If they invest in EVs, the opportunity cost is not improving fuel efficiency in traditional cars.If they focus on petrol cars, they might lose competitiveness in the EV market.

6-Mark Questions

Q11. Analyze why Colombia's economy has a high rate of informal employment.

Lack of formal jobs: The formal sector cannot create enough jobs to absorb the growing labor force.

High barriers to entry: Many jobs in the formal sector require education and specialized skills that low-income workers lack.

Ease of entry into informal jobs: Street vendors, small businesses, and domestic workers face fewer regulations.

Weak enforcement of labor laws: The government struggles to regulate informal businesses.

Agricultural decline: Rural workers migrate to cities but often find low-paying informal jobs instead of formalemployment.

Q12. Discuss how government spending decisions can affect Colombia's economic growth.

Infrastructure investment (Positive Impact): Roads, transport, and digital infrastructure improve business productivity, leading to economic growth.

Education and Healthcare (Positive Impact): More investment in education leads to a skilled workforce, boosting long-term productivity.Better healthcare reduces absenteeism, increasing labor efficiency.

Social Programs (Mixed Impact): Spending on welfare programs reduces poverty but may increase public debt if not managed properly.

Defense Spending (Trade-off): Allocating more funds to military and security might improve stability but reduces spending on economic development projects.

FOUR

Unit 2: The Allocation of Resources

LEARNING OBJECTIVES

LO1: MICRO AND MACRO ECONOMICS-The difference between microeconomics and macroeconomics and the decision makers involved in each.

LO2: ROLE OF MARKET-How a market system works; including buyers, sellers, allocation of scarce resources, market equilibrium, and market disequilibrium. Establishing that the economic problem creates three key questions about determining resource allocation – what to produce, how, and for whom. How the price mechanism provides answers to these key allocation questions.

LO3: DEMAND- Definition, drawing and interpretation of appropriate diagrams. A demand curve to be drawn and used to illustrate movements along a demand curve with appropriate terminology, for example extensions and contractions in demand. The link between individual and market demand in terms of aggregation. The causes of shifts in a demand curve with appropriate terminology, for example increase and decrease in demand.

LO4: SUPPLY-Definition, drawing and interpretation of appropriate diagrams. A supply curve to be drawn and used to illustrate movements along a supply curve with appropriate terminology, for example extensions and contractions in supply. The link between individual and market supply in terms of aggregation. The causes of shifts in a supply curve with appropriate terminology, for example increase and decrease in supply.

LO5: PRICE DETERMINATION- Definition, drawing and interpretation of demand and supply schedules and curves used to establish equilibrium price and sales in a market. Definition, drawing and interpretation of demand and supply schedules and curves used to identify disequilibrium prices and shortages (demand exceeding supply) and surpluses (supply exceeding demand).

LO6: PRICE CHANGES- Changing market conditions as causes of price changes. Demand and supply diagrams to be used to illustrate these changes in market conditions and their consequences for equilibrium price and sales.

LO7: PRICE ELASTICITY OF DEMAND- Calculation of PED using the formula and interpreting the significance of the result. Drawing and interpretation of demand curve diagrams to show different PED. The key influences on whether demand is elastic or inelastic. The relationship between PED and total spending on a product/revenue, both in a diagram and as a calculation. The implications for decision making by consumers, producers and government.

LO8: MARKET ECONOMIC SYSTEMS-definition of market economic system, advantages and disadvantages of the market economic system (including examples of how it works in a variety of different countries.

LO9; MARKET FAILURE- The key terms associated with market failure: public good, merit good, demeritgood, social benefits, external benefits, private benefits, social costs, external costs, private costs. With respect to public goods, merit and demerit goods, external costs and external benefits, abuse of monopolypower and factor immobility. Examples of market failure with respect to these areas only. The implicationsof misallocation of resources in respect of the over consumption of demerit goods and goods with external costs, and the under consumption of merit goods and goods with external benefits. Note: demand and supply diagrams relating to market failure are not required.

LO10: MIXED ECONOMIC SYSTEMS- Definitions, drawing and interpretation of appropriate diagrams showing theeffects of three government microeconomic policy measures: maximum and minimum prices in product, labour and foreign exchange markets; indirect taxation; and subsidies. The implications of other government microeconomic policy measures: regulation; privatisation and nationalisation; and direct provision of goods. The effectiveness of government intervention in overcoming the drawbacks of a market economic system.

TERMS TO REMEMBER

1. **Microeconomics:** The branch of economics that studies individual markets, firms, and consumers.
2. **Macroeconomics:** The study of the entire economy, including inflation, unemployment, and GDP.
3. **Market System:** An economic system where resources are allocated based on supply and demand.
4. **Price Mechanism:** The process by which prices adjust due to changes in supply and demand.
5. **Demand:** The quantity of a good or service consumers are willing and able to buy at different prices.
6. **Law of Demand:** The inverse relationship between price and quantity demanded.
7. **Individual Demand:** The demand of a single consumer for a product.
8. **Market Demand:** The total demand of all consumers in a market.
9. **Movements Along a PPC:** Changes in production levels due to resource reallocation.
10. **Movement Along Demand Curve:** A change in quantity demanded due to price change.
11. **Shift of Demand Curve:** A change in demand due to non-price factors (income, tastes, etc.).
12. **Extension in Demand:** An increase in quantity demanded due to a price fall.
13. **Contraction in Demand:** A decrease in quantity demanded due to a price rise.
14. **Increase in Demand:** A rightward shift of the demand curve due to non-price factors.
15. **Decrease in Demand:** A leftward shift of the demand curve due to non-price factors.
16. **Market Equilibrium:** The point where demand equals supply.
17. **Market Disequilibrium:** A situation where demand and supply are not equal, causing shortages or surpluses.
18. **Supply:** The quantity of a good or service producers are willing and able to sell at different prices.
19. **Law of Supply:** A direct relationship between price and quantity supplied.
20. **Individual Supply:** The supply from a single firm or producer.
21. **Market Supply:** The total supply from all firms in a market.
22. **Increase in Supply:** A rightward shift of the supply curve.
23. **Decrease in Supply:** A leftward shift of the supply curve.
24. **Extension in Supply:** An increase in quantity supplied due to a price rise.
25. **Contraction in Supply:** A decrease in quantity supplied due to a price fall.
26. **Price:** The amount of money required to buy a good or service.
27. **Cost:** The expenses incurred in production.
28. **PED (Price Elasticity of Demand):** Measures how demand responds to price changes.
29. **PED = 1:** Unit elastic demand (proportionate change in quantity and price).
30. **PED > 1:** Elastic demand (quantity demanded changes more than price).
31. **PED < 1:** Inelastic demand (quantity demanded changes less than price).
32. **PED = 0:** Perfectly inelastic demand (no change in quantity).
33. **PED = Infinite:** Perfectly elastic demand (any price increase drops demand to zero).
34. **Revenue:** Total income from selling goods/services (TR = Price × Quantity).
35. **PES (Price Elasticity of Supply):** Measures how supply responds to price changes.
36. **PES = 1:** Unit elastic supply, percentage change in price is equal to percentage change in quantity supplied.
37. **PES > 1: Elastic Supply:** When PES is greater than 1, supply is considered elastic. This means that a small percentage change in price leads to a larger percentage change in quantity supplied.
38. **PES < 1: Inelastic Supply:** When PES is less than 1, supply is inelastic. This means that a percentage change in price results in a smaller percentage change in quantity supplied.
39. **PES = 0: Perfectly Inelastic Supply:** When PES is **zero**, supply is **perfectly inelastic.** This means that quantity supplied remains constant regardless of price changes.

40. **PES = ∞:** Perfectly Elastic Supply: When PES is infinite, supply is perfectly elastic. This means that at a specific price, suppliers are willing to produce and sell an unlimited quantity, but if the price drops even slightly, supply falls to zero.

41. **Market Economic System:** A system where economic decisions are driven by market forces.

42. **Market Failure:** When markets fail to allocate resources efficiently.

43. **Mixed Economic System:** A system combining free markets and government intervention.

44. **Government Intervention:** Actions taken by the government to influence the economy.

45. **Public Good:** A good that is non-rival and non-excludable (e.g., street lighting).

46. **Merit Good:** A good with positive externalities, often under-consumed (e.g., education).

47. **Demerit Good:** A good with negative externalities, often over-consumed (e.g., cigarettes).

48. **Monopoly:** A market with a single dominant seller.

49. **Maximum Price:** A price ceiling set by the government.

50. **Minimum Price:** A price floor set by the government.

51. **Indirect Taxes:** Taxes on goods and services (e.g., VAT).

52. **Subsidy:** Government payments to encourage production/consumption.

53. **Regulation:** Rules imposed by the government to control market activities.

54. **Privatization:** The transfer of public sector firms to private ownership.

55. **Nationalization:** The transfer of private firms to government ownership.

STRUCTURED QUESTIONS

1. How does the price mechanism provide answers to the basic economic problems?[4]

The price mechanism is the system through which prices adjust based on supply and demand, helping to allocate scarce resources efficiently. It addresses the three fundamental economic questions: what to produce, how to produce, and for whom to produce.

For instance, if there is an increase in demand for electric vehicles (EVs) due to rising environmental concerns, the price of EVs will rise, signalling producers like Tesla and BYD to manufacture more. Similarly, firms decide onhow to produce based on costs; if labour becomes expensive, businesses may invest in automation to maintain efficiency. Lastly, the question of for whom to produce is resolved through purchasing power—luxury brands likeRolex cater to high-income consumers, whereas companies like Casio provide affordable watches for the mass market. The price mechanism thus ensures that goods and services are directed toward the areas where they are most needed, promoting efficiency in the economy.

2. Explain two reasons for the leftward shift of the demand curve.[4]

A **leftward shift** in the demand curve means that at every price level, consumers are demanding less of a good or service. This could occur due to several reasons, two of which are:

One major reason is a decrease in consumer income. When people have lower disposable income, they cut back on purchases, particularly for non-essential or luxury goods. For example, during the COVID- 19 pandemic, many people lost their jobs, leading to a decline in demand for travel services, high-end electronics, and designer clothing.

Another cause is a change in consumer preferences, often influenced by technological advancements or changing trends. For instance, the rise of Netflix and Spotify has drastically reduced the demand for DVDs and CDs, shifting the demand curve for physical media to the left. As consumer preferences shift toward more convenient digital alternatives, older products become obsolete, leading to a decline in their demand.

2. How is price elasticity of demand (PED) beneficial to firms and the government?[6]

Understanding price elasticity of demand (PED) is crucial for both firms and governments in making informed economic decisions.

For businesses, knowing whether their product is elastic or inelastic helps them set optimal pricing strategies. If a company like Coca-Cola discovers that demand for its drinks is inelastic, meaning that consumers will continue buying despite price increases, it can raise prices to increase revenue. However, for a product like luxury handbags, which has many substitutes, demand is elastic, and price hikes could lead to a sharp drop in sales.

Governments also use PED to design taxation policies. If they want to raise revenue, they impose higher taxes on goods with inelastic demand, such as petrol, cigarettes, and alcohol, because consumers will continue purchasing despite price increases. In contrast, taxing goods with elastic demand, like luxury goods, may lead to a significant fall in demand, reducing overall tax revenue. Hence, PED plays a vital role in shaping pricing, production, and taxation strategies.

3. Explain two determinants of PED.[6]

Price elasticity of demand is influenced by several factors that determine how much demand changes in response to price variations.

One key determinant is the availability of substitutes. If a product has close substitutes, its demand tends to be elasticbecause consumers can easily switch to alternatives when prices rise. For example, if the price of Pepsiincreases, many consumers may switch to Coca-Cola instead. However, demand for essential medications like insulinremains inelastic, as there are no close substitutes, and patients must continue buying it regardless of price changes.

Another important factor is the proportion of income spent on the good. If a product takes up a large percentage of a consumer's income, demand tends to be elastic. For example, a 20% increase in the price of a chewing gum will have little impact on demand, but a similar increase in the price of a car will significantly affect purchasing decisions, making demand more elastic. The higher the proportion of income spent on a good, the more price- sensitive consumers become.

4. Explain two determinants of PES.[6]

Price elasticity of supply (PES) determines how responsive producers are to price changes.

One significant determinant is spare production capacity. If firms have unused resources, they can quickly increase production when prices rise, making supply more elastic. For example, if Toyota has extra machinery and workers available, it can easily increase car production to meet higher demand. Conversely, industries with limited spare capacity, such as oil refineries, cannot quickly adjust production, making supply inelastic.

Another factor influencing PES is the time period. In the short run, supply is generally inelastic because production adjustments take time. For instance, farmers cannot immediately increase wheat production after a price rise since crops take months to grow. However, in the long run, they can invest in better equipment and expand farmland, making supply more elastic.

5. Explain two significances of PES.[4]

PES is important for both businesses and governments in planning production and policy decisions. For businesses, understanding PES helps firms manage inventory and production efficiently. For example,Apple ensures high PES by keeping extra production capacity for new iPhone launches, allowing it to quickly meet surges in demand and avoid shortages.

For governments, PES influences policy decisions, particularly during emergencies. For example, during theCOVID-19 pandemic, governments needed to ensure an elastic supply of essential medical equipment likeventilators and masks. By providing subsidies and incentives to manufacturers, they helped increase production to meet urgent healthcare needs.

6. Explain two advantages and two disadvantages of the market economic system.[6]

A market economy relies on the forces of supply and demand with minimal government intervention.

One key advantage is efficiency in resource allocation. Since firms aim to maximize profits, they direct resources toward the most in-demand goods and services. For example, tech companies like Google and Amazon thrive because they provide highly valued digital services.

Another advantage is innovation and economic growth. Competition encourages businesses to develop newtechnologies and improve products. Tesla's push for electric vehicles has led competitors to innovate and invest in sustainable energy solutions.

However, a major disadvantage is income inequality. A free market often benefits those with higher skills and capital, leading to disparities. Billionaires like Elon Musk and Jeff Bezos amass vast wealth, while many workers struggle with low wages.

Another downside is market failures, where essential services like healthcare and education may be underprovided. Without government intervention, firms might prioritize profitable activities over social welfare, as seen in the high costs of private healthcare in the US.

7. Explain the causes of market failure.[6]

Market failure occurs when free markets allocate resources inefficiently, leading to negative economic outcomes.

One common cause is negative externalities, where businesses impose costs on society without bearing the consequences. For example, factories polluting rivers create health hazards, but they do not pay for the environmental damage.

Another cause is the under-provision of public goods, which are essential services like street lighting and national defense. Since these goods are non-excludable (available to everyone), private firms have little incentive to provide them, leading to government intervention.

The allocation of resources in an economy is influenced by the price mechanism, elasticity, market structures, and government interventions. While free markets offer efficiency and innovation, market failures require government policies such as taxation, subsidies, and regulations. By balancing market forces and interventions, economies can ensure sustainable and equitable growth.

CASE STUDY: The German Economy

Germany, Europe's largest economy, demonstrates a mixed economic system where both market forces and government intervention play vital roles. The country's economic framework integrates principles of microeconomics and macroeconomics.

The Role of the Market System in Germany

The German economy operates on market principles, where buyers and sellers interact to determine the allocation of scarce resources. The fundamental economic problem—what to produce, how to produce, and for whom to produce—is largely answered by the price mechanism. In industries like automobile manufacturing, companies such as Volkswagen and BMW respond to consumer demand by producing high-quality vehicles while balancing costs through advanced production techniques.

Table 1: Demand schedule of electronic vehicle (EV) in Germany

Price of EV (in €) Quantity Demanded (per 1000 units)

50,000. 10

45,000 15

40,000 30

35,000 40

Table 2: Supply schedule of electronic vehicle (EV) in Germany

Price of EV (in €) Quantity Supplied (per 1000 units)

50,000 50

45,000 40

40,000 30

35,000 15

Questions and answers

2-Mark Questions

1. Define microeconomics.

Answer: Microeconomics is the branch of economics that studies individual consumers, firms, and markets, focusing on how they make decisions about resource allocation, pricing, and production.

2. What is meant by the term 'market failure'?

Answer: Market failure occurs when the free market fails to allocate resources efficiently, leading to overproduction or underproduction of goods and services, such as pollution or under-provision of healthcare.

3-Mark Questions

3. Explain one cause of a shift in the demand curve for electric vehicles in Germany.

Answer: A shift in the demand curve for electric vehicles in Germany can be caused by government subsidies. If the government provides financial incentives for EV purchases, more consumers will be encouraged to buy them, increasing demand and shifting the demand curve to the right.

4. State three advantages of a market economic system.

Efficient resource allocation – Resources are allocated based on supply and demand.

Encourages innovation -Businesses compete to develop better products.

Consumer sovereignty – Consumers have freedom of choice in purchasing goods.

4-Mark Questions

5. Draw and explain the effect of an increase in supply on the equilibrium wage rate.

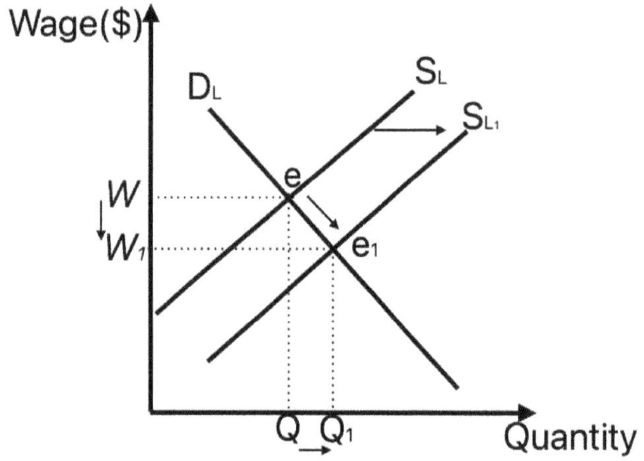

Impact of increase in supply of labour in the labor market

When supply of labour increases, the supply curve shifts to the right from SL to SL1. Equilibrium wage rate in the labour market will falls from W to W1.

6. Explain two reasons why demand for luxury cars in Germany is elastic.

Availability of substitutes – Consumers can switch to cheaper brands if prices increase.

Luxury nature of the good – Luxury cars are not necessities, so consumers can delay or avoid purchases when prices rise.

5-Mark Questions

7. Discuss the impact of indirect taxation on demerit goods in Germany.

Indirecttaxes increase the cost of production, shifting the supply curve to the left. This leads to higher prices and lower quantity demanded. The government aims to reduce consumption of harmful goods, such as cigarettes. However, if demand is inelastic, consumers may continue purchasing despite price increases. The effectiveness depends on the tax rate and consumer responsiveness.

6-Mark Questions

8. Evaluate the effectiveness of government intervention in reducing market failure in Germany.

Government intervention helps correct market failures through policies like subsidies, taxes, and regulations. For example, subsidies for renewable energy promote sustainability, while carbon taxes reduce pollution. Regulations ensure fair competition and prevent monopoly power abuse.However, intervention can lead to inefficiencies if policies are not well-targeted. Overregulationmay discourage businesses, reducing innovation and economic growth. Therefore, a balance is needed to ensure intervention is effective without excessive government control.

9. Calculate PED and PES of EV from 45000 to 40000

PED=percentage change in quantity demanded/percentage change in price

percentage change in quantity demanded=(30-15)/15]X 100=1

percentage change in price=(40000-45000)/40000]X100=12.5

PED=1/12.5

PED=-0.08

PES=percentage change in quantity supplied/percentage change in price

percentage change in quantity supplied=(40-30)/30]X 100=33.33

percentage change in price=(40000-45000)/40000]X100=12.5

PED=33.33/12.5

PED=-2.67

CASE STUDY: The Balance Between Government in Canada

Canada operates as a mixed economy, combining market-driven forces with government intervention to manage economic challenges. With a GDP of $2.14 trillion (2023) and a population of 39 million, the country leverages bothprivate sector competition and public welfare programs to maintain stability. The government plays a crucial role in resource allocation, social services, and regulation to address market failures.

Microeconomics and Macroeconomics in Canada

Canadian farmers decide what crops to grow based on global prices, input costs, and climate conditions. The Bank of Canada influences macroeconomic stability by adjusting interest rates, which stood at 5% in early 2024 to combat inflation.

The Role of Markets in Canada

Canada's economy follows the market system, where buyers and sellers interact to determine prices. Scarce resourcesare allocated based on supply and demand, helping decide what to produce, how to produce, and for whom toproduce. The price mechanism plays a key role, as seen in the housing market, where high demand in cities like Toronto and Vancouver has driven average home prices above $730,000.

The demand for goods and services in Canada depends on income levels, population growth, and consumer preferences. For example, the demand for electric vehicles (EVs) has risen due to government subsidies and rising fuel prices.

Supply depends on production costs, technology, and government policies. The dairy industry, regulated by supply management, limits production to keep prices stable.

Price Determination and Market Equilibrium

In competitive markets, equilibrium price occurs where demand meets supply. In grocery markets, price fluctuations occur based on climate conditions affecting supply.

Table 2: Price Fluctuations in the Canadian Market (2023)

1. Gasoline

Price Change (%) =+12%

Reason-Global oil price hikes

Milk

Price Change=+5%

Reason-Government-regulated pricing

Smartphones

Price change=-8%

Reaon-Increased supply of imports

Price Changes and Market Elasticity

Changes in market conditions affect equilibrium price and quantity. The real estate market is a prime example where rising interest rates reduce affordability, shifting demand downward.

Mixed Economy

In Canada, minimum wage laws play a crucial role in ensuring fair compensation for workers, particularly in low- income sectors. As of 2024, the national minimum wage has increased to $16.65 per hour, helping workers keep pacewith rising living costs. This policy aims to reduce income inequality, boost consumer spending, and improve overalleconomic stability. However, some businesses argue that higher wages may lead to job losses or increased prices for consumers. Additionally, the Canadian government actively supports clean energy initiatives through electric vehicle (EV) subsidies, making eco-friendly transportation more affordable for consumers. These subsidies encourage a shift away from fossil fuels, helping Canada meet its carbon neutrality goals. To further combat climate change, the government has also implemented a carbon tax of $65 per ton of CO_2 emissions, incentivizing businesses to adoptsustainable practices and reduce their environmental impact. While this tax raises costs for industries reliant on fossilfuels, it also generates revenue that can be reinvested in renewable energy projects and climate adaptation strategies. Collectively, these policies reflect Canada's commitment to balancing economic growth, social equity, and environmental sustainability.

Questions and Answers

1. Define the concept of a mixed economy.[2]

Answer: A mixed economy combines elements of both market economies (private sector competition) and planned economies (government intervention) to allocate resources efficiently.

2. Explain how the price mechanism allocates resources in Canada's housing market.[3]

High demand in cities (Toronto, Vancouver) leads to higher prices. Developers respond by building more houses to increase supply.

If supply outpaces demand, prices stabilize, ensuring resource allocation.

3. **Discuss two factors affecting the supply of dairy products in Canada.[4]**

Government Regulation: Canada's supply management system limits production, preventing oversupply andstabilizing prices.

Production Costs: Feed prices, labor wages, and climate conditions impact farmers' ability to produce milk.

4. How does government intervention correct market failures in Canada?[5]

Public Goods Provision: The government provides roads, healthcare, and policing since private firms would underprovide them.

Merit Goods Subsidy: Education and healthcare are subsidized to ensure access for all citizens. Taxation on Demerit Goods: Cigarettes and alcohol have high taxes to discourage consumption. Carbon Tax: The government charges industries per ton of CO_2 emitted to combat climate change.

5. Evaluate the effectiveness of Canada's minimum wage policy in reducing income inequality.[6]

Canada'sminimum wage of $16.65/hour aims to support low-income workers. It has several positive effects, such as:

Higher incomes for workers, reducing poverty levels. Increasedconsumer spending, boosting economic growth. However, it also has drawbacks:

Higher labor costs for businesses may lead to job losses.

Small businesses may struggle to afford higher wages, leading to closures.

Overall, while minimum wages help reduce inequality, additional measures like tax credits and job training programs are needed to fully address income disparity.

FIVE

UNIT 3: MICROECONOMIC DECISION MAKERS

LEARNING OUTCOME

LO1: MONEY AND BANKING-The forms, functions and characteristics of money. The role and importance of central banks and commercial banks for government, producers and consumers.

LO2: HOUSEHOLDS- the influences on spending, saving and borrowing Including income, the rate of interest and confidence – between different households and over time.

LO3: WORKERS-factors affecting an individual's choice of occupation wage and non-wage factors. The influences of demand and supply, relative bargaining power and government policy, including minimum wage on wage determination. Reasons for difference in earnings-how changes in demand and supply, relative bargaining strengths, discrimination and government policy can all influence differences in earnings between workers whether they are: skilled/unskilled; primary/secondary/tertiary; male/female; private sector/public sector. Definition, drawing and interpretation of diagrams that illustrate the effects of changes in demand and supply in the labour market. Division of labor, its advantages and disadvantages for workers, firms and the economy.

LO4: TRADE UNIONS-definition of a trade union, the role of trade unions in the economy, Including engaging in collective bargaining on wages, working hours and working conditions; protecting employment; and influencing government policy. Factors influencing the strength of trade unions. the advantages and disadvantages of trade union activity- From the viewpoint of workers, firms and the government.

LO5: FIRMS- classification of firms, In terms of primary/secondary/tertiary sectors and private/public sector, and therelative size of firms. small firms- The advantages and disadvantages of small firms, the challenges facing small firmsand reasons for their existence. causes and forms of the growth of firms Internal growth, for example increased marketshare. External growth, for example mergers. mergers - Examples, advantages and disadvantages of different types of mergers: horizontal, vertical, and conglomerate. economies and diseconomies of scale - How internal and external economies and diseconomies of scale can affect a firm/industry as the scale of production changes.

LO6: FIRMS AND PRODUCTION- Demand for factors of production Influences to include demand for the product, the price of different factors of production, their availability and their productivity. labour-intensive and capital-intensive production- The reasons for adopting the different forms of production and their advantages and disadvantages. production and productivity - The difference between, and influences on, production and productivity.

LO7: FIRMS COST, REVENUE AND OBJECTIVES- definition of costs of production- Total cost (TC), average totalcost (ATC), fixed cost (FC), variable cost (VC), average fixed cost (AFC), average variable cost (AVC). Total cost(TC), average total cost (ATC), fixed cost (FC), variable cost (VC), average fixed cost (AFC), average variable cost (AVC). calculation of costs of production - TC, ATC, FC, VC, AFC and AVC. Definition, drawing and interpretationof diagrams that show how changes in output affect costs of production. definition of revenue - Total revenue (TR) and average revenue (AR). Note: marginal revenue is not required. calculation of revenue - TR and AR. The influence of sales on revenue. objectives of firms - Survival, social welfare, profit maximisation and growth. [Note: marginal cost and marginal revenue is not required].

LO8: MARKET STRUCTURE- competitive markets- The effect of having a high number of firms on price, quality, choice, profit. monopoly markets- Characteristics, advantages and disadvantages of monopoly. (Diagrams are not required). (The theory of perfect and imperfect competition and diagrams are not required)

TERMS TO REMEMBER

1. **Money** – Any medium of exchange that is widely accepted for goods, services, and repayment of debts. It also serves as a store of value and a unit of account.
2. **Central Banks** – National institutions responsible for monetary policy, issuing currency, regulating commercial banks, and maintaining financial stability. Example: The Federal Reserve (U.S.), Bank of England (U.K.).
3. **Commercial Banks** – Financial institutions that accept deposits, provide loans, and offer financial services to individuals and businesses. Example: JPMorgan Chase, HSBC.
4. **Households** – Economic units consisting of individuals or families who consume goods and services and supply labor to firms.
5. **Spending** – The total amount of money used by individuals, firms, or the government to buy goods and services.
6. **Saving** – The portion of income not spent on consumption but set aside for future use, often in bank accounts or investments.
7. **Borrowing** – The act of obtaining funds from lenders with the obligation to repay with interest over time.
8. **Rate of Interest** – The cost of borrowing money or the return on savings, expressed as a percentage per year.
9. **Workers** – Individuals employed by firms or the government, providing labor in exchange for wages or salaries.
10. **Non-Wage Factors** – Job aspects other than salary that influence employment decisions, such as job security, working conditions, career growth, and work-life balance.
11. **Minimum Wage** – The legally mandated lowest amount an employer can pay a worker per hour or unit of work.
12. **Skilled Workers** – Employees with specialized training or qualifications, such as engineers, doctors, or IT professionals.
13. **Unskilled Workers** – Employees without specialized training, often performing manual labor jobs such as construction or retail work.
14. **Primary Sector** – The part of the economy that extracts natural resources, such as agriculture, fishing, and mining.
15. **Secondary Sector** – The industrial sector that transforms raw materials into finished goods, including manufacturing and construction.
16. **Tertiary Sector** – The services sector that provides intangible goods and services, such as retail, finance, education, and healthcare.
17. **Private Sector** – Businesses and industries owned and operated by individuals or corporations rather than the government.
18. **Public Sector** – Organizations and services funded and operated by the government, such as public schools, healthcare, and national defense.
19. **Labor** – The human effort, both physical and mental, used in the production of goods and services.
20. **Demand for Labor** – The quantity of labor employers are willing to hire at a given wage rate.
21. **Supply of Labor** – The number of workers available and willing to work at different wage levels.
22. **Division of Labor** – The process of breaking down production into different specialized tasks to improve efficiency.
23. **Trade Union** – An organization that represents workers' interests, negotiating better wages, workingconditions, and job security.

24. **Collective Bargaining** – The negotiation process between employers and trade unions to determine wages, benefits, and working conditions.

25. **Firms** – Business entities that produce goods and services in exchange for revenue.

26. **Small Firms** – Businesses with limited market share and workforce. **Advantages**: Flexibility, personal customer service, and innovation. **Disadvantages**: Limited resources, higher costs, and vulnerability to competition.

27. **Internal Growth** – Expansion of a firm through increased production and sales rather than mergers or acquisitions.

28. **Market Share** – The percentage of total sales in an industry controlled by a particular firm.

29. **External Growth** – Expansion of a firm by merging or acquiring other businesses.

30. **Mergers** – The combining of two or more firms to form a larger company.

31. **Horizontal Merger** – A merger between firms in the same industry and production stage. Example: Facebook acquiring Instagram.

32. **Vertical Merger** – A merger between firms at different production stages in the same industry. Example: A car manufacturer acquiring a tire company.

33. **Conglomerate** – A corporation that owns multiple unrelated businesses. Example: General Electric (GE) operates in aviation, healthcare, and finance.

34. **Economies of Scale** – Cost advantages gained by firms as they expand, leading to lower average costs.

35. **Diseconomies of Scale** – Increased production leading to higher costs per unit due to inefficiencies.

36. **Internal Economies of Scale** – Cost savings within a firm due to its growth, such as bulk buying and improved technology.

37. **External Economies of Scale** – Cost advantages gained due to industry growth, such as infrastructure improvements and supplier expansion.

38. **Production** – The process of combining resources to create goods and services.

39. **Productivity** – The efficiency of production, measured as output per unit of input.

40. **Labour-Intensive Production** – Production processes that rely heavily on human labor rather than machines.

41. **Capital-Intensive Production** – Production that relies more on machinery and automation than human labor.

42. **Costs of Production** – Expenses incurred in creating goods and services, including wages, materials, and utilities.

43. **Total Cost (TC)** – The sum of all costs incurred in production (Fixed Cost + Variable Cost).

44. **Average Total Cost (ATC)** – Total cost per unit of output (ATC = TC/Quantity).

45. **Fixed Cost (FC)** – Costs that do not change with output levels, such as rent and salaries.

46. **Variable Cost (VC)** – Costs that vary with production, such as raw materials and wages of hourly workers.

47. **Average Fixed Cost (AFC)** – Fixed cost per unit of output (AFC = FC/Quantity).

48. **Average Variable Cost (AVC)** – Variable cost per unit of output (AVC = VC/Quantity).

49. **Total Revenue (TR)** – The total income from sales (TR = Price × Quantity sold).

50. **Average Revenue (AR)** – Revenue per unit sold (AR = TR/Quantity).

51. **Profit Maximization** – A firm's objective to achieve the highest possible profit by balancing costs and revenues.

52. **Growth** – The expansion of a firm's output, sales, or market share over time.

53. **Market Structure** – The organization and characteristics of different industries, such as the number of firms, competition levels, and pricing power.

54. **Competitive Markets** – Markets with many firms, free entry, and price competition, such as grocery stores.

55. **Price** – The amount of money required to purchase a good or service.
56. **Profit** – The financial gain from business activity (Profit = Total Revenue - Total Cost).
57. **Monopoly** – A market structure where a single firm dominates, limiting competition and controlling prices. Example: Google in search engines.

STRUCTURED QUESTIONS

1. Explain three functions of commercial banks?[6]

Accepting Deposits – Commercial banks provide a safe place for individuals and businesses to deposit their money. They offer different types of accounts, such as savings accounts, current accounts, and fixed deposits, allowing customers to store their money securely while earning interest.

Example: A person deposits their salary into a savings account and earns interest over time.

Providing Loans and Credit – Banks lend money to individuals and businesses for various purposes, such as buying a house, expanding a business, or funding education. They charge interest on these loans, which is a major source of their income.

Example: A business takes a loan from a bank to purchase new machinery, helping it grow and increase production.

Facilitating Payments and Transactions – Commercial banks enable cashless transactions through services such as online banking, credit and debit cards, and electronic fund transfers. They also issue checks and manage payment processing.

Example: A customer pays their electricity bill through online banking, saving time and effort. (6 marks: 2 marks for each function with explanation and example.)

2. Explain three functions of a central bank? [6]

Issuing Currency – The central bank has the exclusive authority to issue the national currency, ensuring a stable and controlled money supply. This helps maintain confidence in the financial system and prevents inflation. Example:The Reserve Bank of India (RBI) prints and regulates the supply of the Indian Rupee to control inflation and economic stability.

Lender of Last Resort – The central bank provides emergency funding to commercial banks facing financial difficulties to prevent bank failures and maintain stability in the banking system. This ensures public confidence and prevents a financial crisis.

Example: During the 2008 financial crisis, the U.S. Federal Reserve provided emergency loans to struggling banks to prevent a collapse of the financial system.

Regulating Commercial Banks – The central bank supervises and regulates commercial banks to ensure financialstability, protect depositors, and prevent risky banking practices. It sets policies on reserve requirements, lending limits, and capital adequacy.

Example: The Bank of England ensures that commercial banks hold a certain percentage of their deposits as reserves to avoid liquidity shortages. *(6 marks: 2 marks for each function with explanation and example.)*

3. Explain three functions of money? [6]

Medium of Exchange – Money is widely accepted as a means of payment for goods and services, eliminating the need for barter, which requires a double coincidence of wants. This makes trade more efficient and convenient.Example: A customer buys groceries using cash or a debit card instead of exchanging goods directly.

Store of Value – Money allows individuals to save their wealth for future use without losing its value over time (unless affected by inflation). This enables people to delay spending and plan for future expenses. Example: A person saves money in a bank account to buy a car next year.

Unit of Account – Money provides a standard measure for pricing goods and services, making it easy to compare values and record financial transactions. This helps in budgeting and economic decision-making.

Example: A laptop priced at $1,000 allows consumers to compare its value with other products, such as a phone priced at $500. (6 marks: 2 marks for each function with explanation and example.)

4. What are two factors that affect spending, saving, and borrowing?

Two key factors that affect spending, saving, and borrowing are:

Interest Rates – Interest rates influence consumer behavior in multiple ways. Higher interest rates make borrowing more expensive, discouraging loans and credit purchases while encouraging saving due to better returns. Conversely, lower interest rates reduce borrowing costs, promoting spending and investments while discouraging saving.

Income Levels – A person's income directly impacts their ability to spend, save, and borrow. Higher income levels enable individuals to allocate more funds toward savings and discretionary spending while also improving their creditworthiness for borrowing. Conversely, lower income limits financial flexibility, often leading toreduced savings and increased reliance on borrowing for essential expenses. (6 marks: Explanation of each factor with clarity and relevance to spending, saving, and borrowing.)

5. What are three factors affecting an individual's choice of occupation?[6]

Three factors affecting an individual's choice of occupation are:

Wage and Salary Levels – The potential earnings from a job significantly influence career decisions.

Higher-paying occupations attract individuals seeking financial stability and growth.

Example: A student choosing between becoming a teacher and a software engineer may opt for software engineering due to its higher salary prospects.

Personal Interests and Skills – People are more likely to choose careers that align with their passions, strengths, and abilities.

Example: An individual with strong mathematical skills and a passion for finance may choose to become an investment banker rather than a graphic designer.

Job Security and Working Conditions – Stability in employment and favorable work environments influence occupational choices. People prefer jobs with long-term security, benefits, and good work-life balance.

Example: A person may choose a government job over a private-sector job due to better job security and retirement benefits. (6 marks: 2 marks for each well-explained factor with relevant examples.)

6. What are two reasons for differences in earnings?[4]

Differences in earnings arise due to various economic and social factors. One major reason is differences in education and skill levels; highly skilled and educated workers typically earn higher wages because their expertise is in high demand. Another factor is variations in demand and supply for specific jobs; occupations thatrequire specialized skills and have a limited labor supply tend to offer higher wages, whereas jobs with an oversupply of workers often pay less.

7. State advantages and disadvantages of specialization of labor?[4]

Advantages of Specialization of Labor:

Increased Productivity – Workers become more skilled and efficient at their tasks, leading to faster production and higher output.

Example: A factory worker assembling only car engines becomes highly proficient, reducing production time and increasing the number of cars produced.

Higher Quality of Work – Specialization allows workers to develop expertise, resulting in better-quality products and services.

Example: A surgeon specializing in heart surgery performs operations with greater precision than a general doctor. Disadvantages of Specialization of Labor:

Job Monotony and Boredom – Repeating the same task daily can lead to dissatisfaction, reducing worker motivation and productivity.

Example: An assembly line worker screwing in bolts all day may feel unfulfilled and disengaged.

Dependence on a Single Skill – If demand for a specialized skill decrease, workers may struggle to find new jobs. *Example:* A typewriter repair specialist may become unemployed as computers replace typewriters. *(4 marks: 1 mark for each advantage and disadvantage, plus 1 mark each for explanation.)*

8. Evaluate specialization of labour. [8]

Specialization of labour offers several benefits, particularly in terms of productivity and efficiency. When workers focus on a specific task, they become highly skilled and proficient, leading to faster production and higher output. For instance, in a car manufacturing plant, workers assigned to specific assembly tasks can complete their work more quickly, contributing to overall efficiency. Additionally, specialization enhances the quality of goods and services since workers develop expertise in their respective areas. A pastry chef who specializes in baking will produce superior-quality cakes compared to a general cook.

Another key advantage of specialization is cost reduction. Businesses save money by minimizing training time and reducing errors, which lowers production costs and increases profitability. Furthermore, specialization encourages innovation, as workers and firms can focus on improving processes and developing new technologies. In industries such as pharmaceuticals and technology, specialization has led to groundbreaking advancements and improved efficiency.

Despite these benefits, specialization has certain drawbacks. One major disadvantage is job monotony, where workersrepeatedly perform the same task, leading to boredom and reduced motivation. For example, an assembly line workertightening screws all day may find the job unfulfilling, which can impact overall productivity. Another risk isoverdependence on a specific skill. If technological advancements make a specialized skill obsolete, workers maystruggle to find new employment. A classic example is the decline of traditional watchmakers as digital watches and smartwatches gained popularity.

Additionally, specialization increases the risk of unemployment and creates interdependence in production. If demand for a specialized product decrease, workers may lose their jobs, as seen in the decline of coal mining due to the shift toward renewable energy. Furthermore, in industries relying on specialized production stages, a delay or failure in one stage can disrupt the entire process. For instance, if a crucial component in a car factory is unavailable, the entire assembly line may come to a halt.

In conclusion, while specialization of labor improves productivity, quality, and efficiency, it also has significantdownsides such as job monotony, unemployment risks, and production dependencies. To maximize its benefits, businesses and workers should focus on continuous skill development and adaptability to remain competitive in a changing job market.

(8 marks: 2 marks for advantages, 2 marks for disadvantages, 2 marks for examples, and 2 marks for a well-structured conclusion.)

9. Evaluate the role of trade unions in the economy?[8]

Trade unions play a significant role in the economy by representing workers' interests and influencing labor market conditions. They negotiate wages and benefits, helping to reduce income inequality and ensuring fair compensation for employees. Additionally, unions advocate for better working conditions, job security, and workplace safety, which enhances productivity and job satisfaction. By promoting skill development and training,they contribute to economic growth and competitiveness. Unions also influence government policies by pushing for labor-friendly laws, such as minimum wages and social security benefits.

However, their actions can sometimes lead to economic disruptions, such as strikes, which may reduce productivity and cause financial losses for businesses. While unions help prevent labour exploitation and ensure fair employment practices, their demands for higher wages and benefits can increase production costs, potentially affecting business competitiveness in global markets. Overall, trade unions play a crucial role in balancing worker rights with economic efficiency, but their influence must be managed to avoid excessive rigidity in labour markets.

In conclusion, while specialization of labour improves productivity, quality, and efficiency, it also has significantdownsides such as job monotony, unemployment risks, and production dependencies. To maximize its benefits, businesses and workers should focus on continuous skill development and adaptability to remain competitive in a changing job market.

(8 marks: 2 marks for advantages, 2 marks for disadvantages, 2 marks for examples, and 2 marks for a well-structured conclusion.)

9. What are two advantages and two disadvantages of trade union activity?[4]

Advantages:

Better Wages and Working Conditions – Trade unions negotiate with employers to secure higher wages, better benefits, and improved working conditions for employees.

Example: In many countries, unions have successfully advocated for minimum wage increases, ensuring fair pay for workers.

Job Security and Legal Protection – Unions help protect workers from unfair dismissals and ensure they receive legal entitlements such as sick leave and pension benefits.

Example: A trade union may intervene if a company attempts to lay off workers without proper compensation. Disadvantages:

Higher Costs for Businesses – Unions often demand higher wages and better benefits, which can increase operational costs for businesses. This may lead to higher consumer prices or job cuts.

Example: A company facing rising labor costs due to union demands may relocate to a country with cheaper labor.

Strikes and Economic Disruptions – Industrial actions such as strikes can halt production and disrupt essential services,negatively impacting the economy.*Example:* A nationwide transport workers' strike can delay goods delivery and affect businesses relying on supply chains. *(4 marks: 1 mark for each advantage and disadvantage, plus 1 mark each for explanation.)*

10. Explain are three characteristics of money?[6]

Three Characteristics of Money

Durability – Money must be long-lasting and resistant to wear and tear so it can be used repeatedly over time.

Example: Coins and banknotes are made from durable materials like metal and polymer to prevent easy damage.

Divisibility – Money should be easily broken down into smaller units to allow for transactions of different values. *Example:* A $100 bill can be exchanged for two $50 bills or ten $10 bills, making it convenient for various purchases.

Portability – Money should be easy to carry and transfer, enabling people to conduct transactions conveniently.

Example: Banknotes and digital money allow individuals to make purchases without carrying bulky goods for trade.

(6 marks: 2 marks for each characteristic with explanation and example.)

11. Evaluate how do changes in demand and supply, relative bargaining strengths, discrimination, andgovernment policy influence differences in earnings between skilled and unskilled workers?[8]

Earnings differences between skilled and unskilled workers are influenced by several key factors, including demand and supply, bargaining power, discrimination, and government policies.

One of the most significant factors is changes in demand and supply. Skilled workers are often in higher demand due to their specialized expertise, while the supply of skilled labor is limited because of the time and cost required for training. This results in higher wages for skilled workers. In contrast, unskilled workers are more abundant, leading to lower wages. For example, doctors and engineers earn significantly more than retail workers or manual laborers due to the demand for their expertise and the limited supply of qualified professionals.

Relative bargaining strength also plays a crucial role in wage differences. Skilled workers, especially those in unions orprofessional associations, have greater bargaining power and can negotiate for higher salaries and better working conditions. Unskilled workers, on the other hand, often lack collective bargaining power, making them more vulnerable to low wages and poor working conditions. For instance, software engineers in large tech companies can negotiate competitive salaries, while fast-food workers may have little influence over their wages.

Discrimination in the labor market can further contribute to wage disparities. Certain groups, such as women, ethnic minorities, or individuals from disadvantaged backgrounds, may face wage discrimination, even if they possess the same skills as others. This can lead to lower earnings for equally qualified workers. For example, studies have shown that in some countries, women are often paid less than men for performing the same skilled jobs, despite having similar qualifications and experience.

Lastly, government policies can either reduce or widen earnings differences between skilled and unskilled workers. Minimum wage laws, progressive taxation, and education subsidies can help narrow wage gaps by ensuring fair payand increasing access to skill development. However, if policies favor businesses over workers or fail to regulate unfair labor practices, income inequality may persist. For example, governments that invest in vocational training programs help unskilled workers gain new skills and access higher-paying jobs, reducing wage gaps over time.

Conclusion

Earnings differences between skilled and unskilled workers are shaped by multiple factors. While demand and supply,bargaining power, and discrimination often lead to wage disparities, government policies can play a crucial role in reducing these gaps. Ensuring fair wages and access to education and training opportunities is essential for promoting economic equality and improving living standards for all workers.

(8 marks: 2 marks for demand and supply, 2 marks for bargaining power, 2 marks for discrimination and government policy, and 2 marks for a well-structured conclusion.)

12. Evaluate the factors influence differences in earnings between workers in the primary, secondary, and tertiary sectors?[8]

Earnings vary significantly across the primary (agriculture, fishing, mining), secondary (manufacturing, construction), and tertiary (services, finance, healthcare) sectors due to several key factors, including demand and supply, skill level, working conditions, productivity, and government policies.

One major factor is skill level and education requirements. Jobs in the tertiary sector often require higher levels of education and specialized skills, leading to higher wages. For instance, doctors, lawyers, and financial analysts typically earn more than factory workers or farmers because their jobs require advanced training. In contrast,primary sector jobs, such as farming and fishing, generally require fewer qualifications, resulting in lower earnings.

Working conditions and job risks also affect wages. Many primary sector jobs involve physically demanding labor and exposure to harsh environments, yet wages remain low due to the availability of unskilled labor. Secondary sectorjobs,such as factory work, may offer slightly better wages but still involve repetitive tasks and health risks. Tertiary sector jobs, especially in professional fields, often provide safer working conditions, job security, and better benefits,leading to higher earnings. However, some service jobs, such as retail and hospitality, may still offer low wages despite being in the tertiary sector.

Demand and supply of labour play a crucial role as well. As economies develop, there is greater demand for tertiary sector workers due to growth in finance, technology, and healthcare, leading to higher wages. Meanwhile, the primary sector often faces oversupply of labour, especially in developing countries, keeping wages low. Thesecondary sector experiences wage fluctuations depending on industrial demand, automation, and outsourcing. For example, manufacturing workers in high-tech industries may earn well, while those in low-skilled assembly line jobs may receive lower wages.

Government policies and globalization also influence wage differences. In many developed countries, the governmentsupports agriculture and mining with subsidies, but wages in these industries remain low due to global competition. In contrast, governments often invest in education and infrastructure, boosting wages in the tertiary sector. Globalization has also led to outsourcing of manufacturing jobs to lower-cost countries, reducing earnings for some secondary sector workers while increasing opportunities in the tertiary sector.

Conclusion

Earnings differences across the primary, secondary, and tertiary sectors are influenced by skill requirements, working conditions, demand and supply, and government policies. In general, the tertiary sector offers the highest wages due to greater specialization and demand for skilled workers, while the primary sector often has the lowest wages due tolabour oversupply and difficult working conditions. However, variations exist within each sector, and government intervention can help reduce wage disparities and improve living standards.

(8 marks: 2 marks for skill level, 2 marks for working conditions, 2 marks for demand and government influence, and 2 marks for a well-structured conclusion.)

13. Evaluate the factors influence differences in earnings between male and female workers?[8]

Earnings differences between male and female workers are influenced by several key factors, including education and skill levels, occupational segregation, discrimination, work experience, and government policies.

One of the primary factors is education and skill level. While educational opportunities for women have improved globally, in some regions, men still have greater access to higher education and specialized training, leading to better-paying job opportunities. For example, men are more likely to enter high-paying fields such as engineering and finance, while women are often concentrated in lower-paid sectors like teaching and caregiving.

Occupational segregation also plays a major role in wage disparities. Women are often overrepresented in low- payingindustries, while men dominate high-paying technical and leadership roles. This "gendered division of labor" contributesto wage gaps. For instance, in many countries, male-dominated fields such as construction and IT tend to offer higher salaries than female-dominated sectors like retail and hospitality.

Another significant factor is work experience and career interruptions. Women are more likely than men to take career breaks for childcare and family responsibilities, leading to lower accumulated work experience and slower careerprogression. This results in fewer promotions and lower lifetime earnings. For example, a woman who takes a fewyears off for maternity leave may struggle to re-enter the workforce at the same level as her male counterparts.

Workplace discrimination and gender biases further contribute to earnings differences. Despite having similar qualifications and experience, women often face wage discrimination, with employers offering them lower salaries than men for the same job. Additionally, the "glass ceiling" effect prevents many women from reaching senior management positions, limiting their earning potential. Studies have shown that even in high-paying professions, such as law and medicine, women tend to earn less than men due to biased hiring and promotion practices.

Government policies and labor laws can help reduce or widen gender wage gaps. In some countries, equal pay laws andparental leave policies support women's participation in the workforce, reducing earnings disparities. However, inplaces where such protections are weak or poorly enforced, wage inequality persists. For example, Scandinavian countries, which have strong policies promoting workplace gender equality, have smaller wage gaps compared to countries with fewer protections.

Conclusion

Earnings differences between male and female workers are shaped by multiple factors, including education, occupational segregation, career interruptions, discrimination, and government policies. While progress has been made in narrowing the gender wage gap, disparities still exist in many industries and regions. Addressing these issues requires stronger legal protections, equal access to education, and workplace policies that promote gender equality and career advancement opportunities for women.

(8 marks: 2 marks for occupational segregation, 2 marks for work experience and discrimination, 2 marks for government influence, and 2 marks for a well-structured conclusion.)

14. What factors influence differences in earnings between public and private sector workers? [4]

The earnings of public and private sector workers differ due to several factors. Government policy plays a major role in setting wages for public sector workers, ensuring job security and benefits, even if salaries may be lower compared to equivalent private-sector jobs. In contrast, relative bargaining power in the private sector may lead to higher wages, particularly for skilled employees who negotiate better salaries. Demand and supply also influence wages; in industries where private-sector jobs are more competitive, wages tend to be higher. However, public sector jobs often offer better long-term stability, pensions, and other benefits, compensating for the potential wage gap.

15. What are three factors influencing the strength of trade unions?[4]

The effectiveness of trade unions depends on several factors. Firstly, membership size is crucial—larger unions have more bargaining power to negotiate with employers. Secondly, government legislation influences union strength;strong legal protections enhance union rights, while restrictive laws weaken their influence. Lastly,economic conditions play a role—during economic downturns, unions may struggle to demand higher wages, while in periods of growth, they can secure better benefits for workers.

16. Evaluate that small firms are required in an economy.[8]

Small firms play a crucial role in an economy by contributing to employment, innovation, and competition. However, they also face challenges such as limited resources and difficulty competing with large firms.

One of the key benefits of small firms is job creation. Small businesses employ a significant portion of the workforce,especially in developing economies where large corporations are scarce. They provide opportunities for entrepreneurship and self-employment, reducing unemployment rates. For example, many small retail shops and local service providers help sustain livelihoods in rural areas.

Another advantage is innovation and flexibility. Small firms are often more adaptable to changing market conditions and can introduce innovative products and services faster than large firms. Many technological breakthroughs and successful startups began as small businesses. For instance, companies like Apple and Amazon started as small firms before growing into global giants.

Additionally, small firms contribute to market competition and consumer choice. They help prevent monopolies by offering alternatives to products and services provided by large corporations. This competition leads to better quality, lower prices, and improved customer service. For example, small local restaurants often provide unique dining experiences that challenge large fast-food chains.

However, small firms also face significant challenges. Limited access to finance is a major drawback, as banks and investors may be hesitant to provide funding due to the higher risks involved. This can make it difficult for small businesses to expand and compete with larger firms.

Furthermore, economies of scale favor large firms, which can produce goods and services at lower costs due to bulk purchasing, advanced technology, and better infrastructure. Small firms, on the other hand, often struggle with high production costs and may charge higher prices, making them less competitive.

Conclusion

Small firms are essential for economic growth, employment, innovation, and competition. However, they face challenges such as financial constraints and competition from larger firms. Government support through favorable policies, financial assistance, and infrastructure development can help small businesses thrive and contribute effectively to the economy.

(8 marks: 2 marks for job creation, 2 marks for innovation and competition, 2 marks for challenges, and 2 marks for a well-structured conclusion.)

17. What is one advantage and one disadvantage of different types of mergers?[6]

Horizontal mergers (between firms in the same industry): Advantage—economies of scale, leading to cost savings; Disadvantage—reduced competition, which may result in higher prices.

Vertical mergers (between suppliers and producers): Advantage—greater control over the supply chain, reducing costs and delays; Disadvantage—less flexibility, as companies may struggle to switch suppliers.

Conglomerate mergers (between unrelated businesses): Advantage—diversification, reducing business risk;Disadvantage—management difficulties, as firms may lack expertise in the new industry.

18. How do internal and external economies and diseconomies of scale affect firms as production scales up?[6]

As firms expand production, they experience economies of scale, which reduce costs per unit, and diseconomies of scale, which increase costs. These effects can be internal (within the firm) or external (within the industry or economy).

Internal Economies of Scale – As a firm grows, it benefits from lower costs due to increased efficiency. These include technical, managerial, financial, and purchasing economies.

Example: A car manufacturer can buy raw materials in bulk at a lower price, reducing costs per unit.

External Economies of Scale – When an entire industry grows, firms within it benefit from lower costs due to shared infrastructure, skilled labor, and supplier networks.

Example: Technology firms in Silicon Valley benefit from a pool of skilled workers and specialized suppliers, reducing recruitment and training costs.

Diseconomies of Scale – As firms grow too large, inefficiencies may arise, leading to higher costs. Internal diseconomies include management difficulties, communication problems, and worker dissatisfaction. External diseconomies occur when industry growth leads to resource shortages or congestion.

Example: A large corporation may face slower decision-making and increased bureaucracy, reducing efficiency. Similarly, too many firms in one location may lead to higher wages and rent, increasing costs.

Conclusion

Economies of scale help firms reduce costs and gain a competitive advantage as production expands. However, if afirm or industry grows too large, diseconomies of scale can lead to inefficiencies and rising costs, limiting further growth. Firms must manage expansion carefully to maximize benefits while minimizing inefficiencies.

(6 marks: 2 marks for internal economies, 2 marks for external economies, and 2 marks for diseconomies of scale, with examples.)

19. Differentiate between labour-intensive and capital-intensive production techniques.[6]

Labor-intensive production relies more on human labor than machinery, making it suitable for industries where manual skills are essential. It typically involves high labor costs but lower machinery costs, making it common in sectors such as agriculture, textile production, and handmade crafts. This technique is particularly beneficial in developing countries where labor is abundant and relatively inexpensive, providing more employment opportunities. However, it may be less efficient for large-scale production compared to automated processes.

On the other hand, capital-intensive production depends more on machinery and advanced technology than human labor. This method is widely used in industries like car manufacturing, oil refining, and automated factories, where high investment in equipment leads to lower labor costs and increased efficiency. While capital-intensive production is more suitable for large-scale operations, it can reduce employment opportunities as automation replaces manual work. It is commonly found in developed economies with better access to technology and financial resources.

In conclusion, labor-intensive production is ideal for businesses requiring significant human input, whereas capital- intensive production is more effective for industries prioritizing automation and efficiency. The choice between these techniques depends on factors such as cost, efficiency, and resource availability in a given economy.

(6 marks: 2 marks for defining labor-intensive production, 2 marks for defining capital-intensive production, and 2 marks for a well-structured comparison and conclusion.)

20. What are the effects of having a high number of firms in an industry on price, quality, choice, and profit? [6]

When an industry has a high number of firms, it creates strong competition, which affects price, quality, choice, and profit in various ways.

Firstly, prices tend to decrease due to intense competition among firms. Each business tries to attract customers by offering lower prices, leading to more affordable products and services for consumers. For example, in the smartphone industry, multiple brands compete by reducing prices to gain market share.

Secondly, product quality generally improves because firms must differentiate themselves to attract customers. Businesses invest in better materials, innovation, and customer service to gain a competitive edge. For instance, competition in the automobile industry pushes manufacturers to improve safety features and fuel efficiency.

Thirdly, consumer choice expands as firms offer a wide variety of products and services to stand out in the market. Different brands provide various designs, features, and price ranges, giving consumers more options. For example, in the fashion industry, multiple brands offer diverse clothing styles to cater to different tastes and budgets.

However, profits for individual firms tend to decline because intense competition reduces the ability to charge high prices. Businesses must operate efficiently and manage costs carefully to remain profitable. Some firms may struggle to survive, especially smaller ones with fewer resources. For example, in the airline industry, low-cost carriers face pressure to keep fares low, limiting profit margins.

Conclusion

A high number of firms in an industry benefits consumers through lower prices, better quality, and increased choice. However, for firms, competition reduces profit margins, making it challenging to sustain long-term success. To survive, businesses must innovate, reduce costs, and build strong brand loyalty.

(6 marks: 1.5 marks for each factor—price, quality, choice, and profit—with explanation and examples.)

21. What are the characteristics, advantages, and disadvantages of monopolies?

Two Characteristics of Monopolies

Single Seller – A monopoly exists when a single firm dominates the entire market, meaning there are no direct competitors. This firm controls supply and pricing decisions.

Example: Google dominates the search engine market, facing little competition.

High Barriers to Entry – Monopolies have significant obstacles preventing new firms from entering the market, such as high startup costs, legal restrictions, or control over key resources.

Example: Utility companies, like electricity providers, often require government licenses, making it difficult for new firms to compete. *(2 marks: 1 mark for each characteristic.)*

22. Evaluate whether monopolies are good for the economy. [8]

Monopolies have both advantages and disadvantages, making their overall impact on the economy a subject of debate.

One of the key benefits of monopolies is economies of scale, which allow large firms to produce goods and services at lower costs. Since a monopoly controls the entire market, it can invest in advanced technology, research, and development, leading to innovation and efficiency. For example, pharmaceutical monopolies can afford to spend billions on drug development, benefiting society with life-saving medicines.

Another advantage is stability and long-term investment. Without the pressure of competition, monopolies can focus on improving their products and expanding infrastructure. This is especially important in industries such as utilities, where large-scale investments in electricity grids or water supply systems are needed.

However, monopolies also have several drawbacks. A major concern is higher prices and reduced consumer choice. Since there are no competitors, monopolists can charge higher prices without fear of losing customers. This leads tolower consumer welfare, as people may be forced to buy expensive products or services. For example, in regions with only one internet provider, customers often pay high fees for limited-service quality.

Furthermore, monopolies may become less efficient over time due to the lack of competition. Without rivals, there is little motivation to improve productivity, reduce costs, or enhance customer service. This can result in poor- quality products and inefficiency, as seen in some government-controlled monopolies where service delays and bureaucracy are common.

Conclusion

Monopolies can be beneficial when they lead to economies of scale, innovation, and long-term investment, particularly in industries requiring heavy infrastructure. However, they often lead to higher prices, reduced efficiency,and limited consumer choice. To balance these effects, governments may regulate monopolies by setting price controls, promoting fair competition, or breaking them up when they become too powerful.

(8 marks: 2 marks for benefits, 2 marks for drawbacks, 2 marks for examples, and 2 marks for a well-structured conclusion.)

CASE STUDY: The Role of Banking, Households, and Market Structures in the United States

The United States serves as an ideal case study for analyzing the dynamics of money and banking, household financial behavior, labor markets, trade unions, firms, production, costs, revenue, and market structures. As the world's largest economy, the U.S. has a complex financial system, diverse employment sectors, and a range of market structures that influence economic activity. The financial sector, labor force, and firms in the U.S. collectively shape its economic growth and stability, providing valuable insights into how modern economies function.

Money in the U.S. exists in multiple forms, including physical currency, demand deposits, and digital money. The functions of money, such as serving as a medium of exchange, a store of value, and a unit of account, are vital in ensuring economic stability. The U.S. Federal Reserve (Fed) plays a central role in regulating monetary policy, stabilizing inflation, and ensuring liquidity in financial markets. It controls the money supply, adjusts interest rates, and acts as a lender of last resort during financial crises. Commercial banks such as JPMorgan Chase, Bank of America,and Wells Fargo provide credit and banking services to consumers and businesses, influencing economic activity. During the 2008 financial crisis, the Fed introduced measures like quantitative easing to stabilize the economy, demonstrating the critical role of central banks in preventing financial collapse and ensuring liquidity.

Household spending, saving, and borrowing behavior in the U.S. are influenced by factors such as income levels, interest rates, and consumer confidence. In times of economic growth, households tend to increase spending due to rising incomes and job security. However, during recessions, such as the 2008 financial crisis and the COVID-19 pandemic, many households reduced spending and increased saving due to uncertainty. The Fed's decision to lower interest rates during these periods encouraged borrowing, particularly for mortgages and auto loans. Over time, the risein student loan debt has become a significant issue, affecting millennials' ability to purchase homes and invest in long-term assets. The wealth gap between high-income and low-income households continues to widen due to variations insavings rates, investment opportunities, and access to credit, further highlighting disparities in financial security.

The choice of occupation for workers in the U.S. is shaped by both wage and non-wage factors such as working conditions, job security, and benefits. The labor market is influenced by demand and supply dynamics, bargaining power, and government policies, including minimum wage laws. For instance, the federal minimum wage has remained at $7.25 per hour since 2009, though states like California and New York have implemented higher minimum wages to reflect living costs. Wage disparities exist due to factors such as skills, education, and sectoral employment. Tech sector workers in Silicon Valley earn significantly higher wages than unskilled laborers in retail or manufacturing. Gender wage gaps also persist, with women earning approximately 82 cents for every dollar earned by men, according to the U.S. Bureau of Labor Statistics. Additionally, the employment structure varies across industries, with higher wages in finance, healthcare, and technology compared to agriculture and service- based occupations.

Trade unions in the U.S. play a crucial role in advocating for better wages, working conditions, and employee rights. Historically, organizations like the United Auto Workers (UAW) and the American Federation of Labor (AFL) have fought for collective bargaining rights. However, union membership has declined over the years, with only 10.3% of workers being unionized in 2021. Despite this, unions have achieved significant victories, such as the recent laborstrikes by Amazon warehouse workers advocating for improved wages and working conditions. While unions benefit workers by securing better pay and job security, firms often argue that high union wages increase production costs, reducing competitiveness. Government policies regarding labor laws and union rights continue to influence the bargaining power of workers and their ability to negotiate for better benefits.

The U.S. economy comprises firms operating in primary, secondary, and tertiary sectors, with a strong presence in bothprivate and public sectors. Small firms play a vital role in innovation and job creation, but they face challenges such as limited access to capital and competition from large corporations. For example, independent bookstores struggle tocompete with Amazon's pricing and logistics. Firms grow through internal expansion (increasing market share) andexternal expansion via mergers. The merger between Disney and 21st Century Fox in 2019 is an example of a horizontalmerger, while Tesla's acquisition of SolarCity represents a vertical merger. These mergers enhance market power but may also lead to reduced competition. Larger firms often achieve economies of scale, lowering costs through mass production and increased efficiency, but excessive market concentration can limit consumer choices and drive up prices.

Firms require factors of production such as labor, land, capital, and entrepreneurship. Industries in the U.S. adopt either labor-intensive or capital-intensive production depending on their needs. The agricultural sector relies heavily on labor-intensive methods, while the automobile industry is capital-intensive, using advanced robotics for production. Productivity in the U.S. economy is driven by technological advancements, with firms like Tesla and Apple investingheavily in automation and research to enhance efficiency. Innovations in artificial intelligence and automation continueto reshape industries, increasing efficiency while also raising concerns about job displacement.

Understanding costs is crucial for firms in the U.S. to achieve profitability. Fixed costs, such as rent and salaries, and variable costs, such as raw materials, impact total production costs. Firms aim to maximize revenue by optimizing pricing strategies. Total revenue (TR) is calculated as price multiplied by quantity sold, while average revenue (AR) represents revenue per unit. Amazon's pricing strategy demonstrates how firms adjust prices to maximize sales volume while maintaining profitability. Objectives of firms range from survival in competitive markets to profitmaximization and social responsibility. For example, Google invests in renewable energy projects as part of its corporate social responsibility initiatives. Balancing profitability with sustainable business practices remains a key challenge for modern corporations.

The U.S. economy exhibits various market structures, including competitive markets and monopolies. Competitive markets, such as the fast-food industry, consist of numerous firms offering similar products, leading to price competition and consumer choice. In contrast, monopolies like Google's dominance in the online search industry raise concerns about reduced consumer choice and higher prices. While monopolies benefit from economies of scale, theymay also lead to reduced innovation due to lack of competition. Government regulations, such as antitrust laws, aim to prevent monopolistic practices and promote market fairness. The ongoing scrutiny of big tech companies by regulatorshighlights the tensions between market dominance, consumer rights, and fair competition.

Answer the following questions:

Mark Questions:

1. What are the three primary functions of money?

The three primary functions of money are:

Medium of exchange

Store of value

Unit of account

2. Which central bank regulates monetary policy in the U.S.?

The U.S. Federal Reserve (Fed) regulates monetary policy.

3. Name any two commercial banks in the U.S.

JPMorgan Chase and Bank of America.

4. What is the current federal minimum wage in the U.S.?

$7.25 per hour (since 2009).

5. Which sector is highly capital-intensive in the U.S.?

The automobile industry.

6. What does TR (Total Revenue) stand for?

TR stands for Total Revenue, calculated as Price × Quantity Sold.

2-Mark Questions:

7. How did the Federal Reserve respond to the 2008 financial crisis?

The Federal Reserve introduced quantitative easing and lowered interest rates to stabilize the economy and ensure liquidity.

8. What role do trade unions play in the U.S. labor market?

Trade unions advocate for better wages, working conditions, and employee rights through collective bargaining and labor strikes.

9. How does a monopoly impact consumer choice?

A monopoly reduces consumer choice by limiting competition, potentially leading to higher prices and decreased innovation.

10. Why do some states have higher minimum wages than the federal level?

States like California and New York set higher minimum wages to reflect the cost of living in their regions.

11. What is the impact of high union wages on firms?

High union wages increase production costs, potentially reducing firms' competitiveness.

12. Define economies of scale with an example.

Economies of scale refer to cost advantages firms achieve as production increases. Example: Amazon lowers costs through mass production and efficient logistics.

3-Mark Questions:

13. Explain the impact of interest rates on household borrowing.

Lower interest rates encourage borrowing for mortgages, auto loans, and investments, stimulating economic growth. Conversely, higher interest rates reduce borrowing and increase saving.

14. Why is student loan debt a concern in the U.S.?

Rising student loan debt affects millennials' ability to buy homes and invest in long-term assets, widening wealth inequality.

15. How do firms grow through mergers? Provide examples.

Firms grow through horizontal mergers (e.g., Disney and 21st Century Fox) and vertical mergers (e.g., Tesla acquiring SolarCity), increasing market power and efficiency.

16. What are the key differences between labor-intensive and capital-intensive industries?

Labor-intensive industries rely more on human labor (e.g., agriculture), while capital-intensive industries use advanced machinery and automation (e.g., automobile industry).

17. How does technological advancement influence productivity in the U.S.?

Innovations in AI and automation improve efficiency and reduce costs, but they also raise concerns about job displacement.

18. Describe the impact of wealth disparity on household financial security.

High-income households save and invest more, widening the wealth gap, while low-income households struggle with limited access to credit and financial stability.

4-Mark Questions:

19. Discuss the role of the Federal Reserve in stabilizing the U.S. economy.

The Federal Reserve controls the money supply, adjusts interest rates, and acts as a lender of last resort. Duringfinancial crises, it implements measures like quantitative easing to stabilize inflation and liquidity.

20. Explain how government policies influence the labor market.

Government policies such as minimum wage laws, labor protections, and union rights impact wages, job security, and employment dynamics in various industries.

21. What are the advantages and disadvantages of monopolies?

Advantages: Monopolies benefit from economies of scale and invest in innovation. Disadvantages:They limit consumer choice, reduce competition, and may lead to higher prices.

22. How does consumer confidence impact household spending?

High consumer confidence leads to increased spending and economic growth. In contrast, uncertainty during recessions (e.g., COVID-19) causes reduced spending and higher savings.

6-Mark Questions:

23. Analyze the impact of market structures on competition in the U.S. economy.

The U.S. economy exhibits various market structures, influencing competition. Competitive markets (e.g., fast food) encourage price competition and innovation, benefiting consumers. Monopolies (e.g., Google) dominate their sectors,raising concerns about reduced consumer choice and higher prices. Government regulations, such as antitrust laws, aim to ensure fair competition. Mergers and acquisitions further shape market dynamics, with some firms gaining excessive power. Balancing competition with efficiency remains a key challenge.

24. Evaluate the significance of the financial sector in the U.S. economy.

The financial sector plays a crucial role in economic growth. The Federal Reserve regulates monetary policy, ensuring stability. Commercial banks provide credit and investment opportunities, influencing business expansion and consumer spending. During crises (e.g., 2008 financial crisis), the financial sector's stability is vital in preventing economic collapse. However, issues like wealth disparity and excessive corporate influence raise concerns about financial inclusivity.

25. How do firms balance profit maximization with social responsibility? Provide examples.

Firms aim to maximize profits while maintaining social responsibility. Companies like Google invest in renewable energy to support sustainability. Amazon optimizes pricing to attract consumers while maintaining profitability. However, some firms prioritize profits over ethical considerations, leading to labor exploitation and environmental concerns. Government regulations and consumer awareness push firms toward ethical practic

CASE STUDY

The Role of Banking, Households, and Market Structures in China

China, as the world's second-largest economy, has undergone an impressive transformation from a centrally planned system to a more market-oriented economy. However, state intervention remains a key feature of its financial and industrial sectors. The country's banking system, household financial behavior, labor market dynamics, and market structures significantly influence its economic growth and stability. This case study explores these elements, highlighting their impact on China's long-term economic trajectory.

The Role of Banking and Monetary Policy in China

China's banking system is dominated by state-owned banks, with institutions such as the Industrial and Commercial Bank of China (ICBC), Bank of China (BOC), China Construction Bank (CCB), and Agricultural Bank of China (ABC) controlling the majority of financial transactions. The People's Bank of China (PBOC) serves as the central authority, regulating interest rates and monetary policies.

Unlike Western economies, China follows a dual-interest rate system, where state directives influence lending more than market forces. The PBOC adjusts reserve ratios and liquidity injections to control inflation and economic growth. For example, in 2023, the PBOC lowered the reserve requirement ratio (RRR) by 0.25%, injecting liquidity into the banking system to support businesses post-COVID.

The rise of digital banking and fintech has also transformed financial transactions in China. Alipay and WeChatPay dominate digital payments, handling over $47 trillion in transactions in 2022. The introduction of the Digital Yuan (e-CNY) marks China's first step toward a fully state-controlled digital currency.

Consumption Patterns

Chinese households traditionally have high savings rates, averaging over 30% of disposable income, compared to 6-8% in the U.S. This is driven by a lack of strong social security benefits, high healthcare and education costs, and cultural factors emphasizing wealth accumulation for future generations.

The real estate sector is central to household wealth accumulation, with 90% of urban Chinese households owning property. However, the Evergrande debt crisis exposed weaknesses in speculative real estate investments, leading to a government crackdown on over-leveraged property developers.

Consumer debt in China has been rising, particularly in platforms mortgages, auto loans, and online credit. The household debt-to-GDP ratio has surged to 62%, reflecting an increasing reliance on credit-driven consumption.

Labor Markets in China

China's labor market has transitioned from low-wage manufacturing jobs to a high-skilled technology- driven economy. While urban wages have risen by an average of 8% annually, rural-urban income disparities remain a concern. The minimum wage varies by region, with Shanghai offering 2,590 yuan ($400) per month, while less developed provinces offer much lower wages.

Trade unions in China operate under state control, with the All-China Federation of Trade Unions (ACFTU)representing workers. Despite government restrictions on independent labor movements, recent protests in the technology and gig economy sectors have drawn attention to excessive work hours and wage inequalities.

Market Structures in China

China's industrial landscape consists of state monopolies, private oligopolies, and highly competitive markets. Energy, telecommunications, and banking remain dominated by state-owned enterprises (SOEs), while sectors like e-commerce and consumer goods are more competitive.

The "Made in China 2025" strategy seeks to reduce dependency on foreign technology by investing in semiconductors, artificial intelligence, and electric vehicles (EVs). Companies like Huawei and BYD areleading the charge in technological innovation, backed by state support. However, recent antitrust regulationson big tech firms like Alibaba and Tencent reflect the government's push for a more balanced competitive environment.

Answer the following questions:

1-Mark Questions

Q1: **Which Chinese institution controls the country's monetary policy?**

The People's Bank of China (PBOC) controls China's monetary policy.

2-Mark Questions

Q2: Name two major digital payment platforms in China and their parent companies.

Alipay (owned by Ant Group) WeChat Pay (owned by Tencent)

3-Mark Questions

Q3: Explain why Chinese households have a higher savings rate compared to Western economies.

Chinese households tend to save more due to:

Limited social security benefits, requiring individuals to self-fund retirement and healthcare expenses.

High education costs, compelling families to save for children's schooling and tuition fees.

Cultural factors, where wealth accumulation is considered essential for family stability and future generations.

4-Mark Questions

Q4: How does the People's Bank of China (PBOC) regulate the economy differently from the U.S. Federal Reserve?

The PBOC uses reserve requirements, loan quotas, and liquidity injections to regulate the economy, whereas theU.S. Federal Reserve relies on interest rate adjustments and open market operations. Additionally, China follows a dual-interest rate system, meaning both state directives and market forces influence lending.

Q5: What led to the Evergrande real estate crisis, and how did it impact the Chinese economy?

The Evergrande crisis was caused by excessive debt accumulation, over-leveraged projects, and regulatory tightening under the "Three Red Lines" policy. Its impact included:

A decline in property sales, leading to lower construction activity.

Increased financial risk for banks and investors exposed to Evergrande's debts.

Government intervention, forcing restructuring to prevent economic instability.

Q6: What are the key goals of the "Made in China 2025" policy?

The "Made in China 2025" policy aims to:

Reduce reliance on foreign technology.

Develop advanced manufacturing industries, such as semiconductors, AI, and electric vehicles. Strengthen China's global competitiveness in high-tech sectors.

Increase domestic innovation and R&D investment.

6-Mark Questions

Q7: Compare China's banking system with that of the United States.

Ownership: China's banking system is state-dominated, while the U.S. has a privately driven banking sector.

Regulation: The PBOC controls lending quotas and monetary **policy**, whereas the U.S. Federal Reserve **uses** open market operations and interest rate adjustments.

Lending Focus: Chinese banks prioritize state-owned enterprises (SOEs), while U.S. banks focus on private sector and small businesses.

Digital Payments: China leads in mobile transactions (85% of payments), whereas the U.S. still relies on credit and debit cards.

Q8: Discuss the impact of China's labor market transformation on wages and employment.

China's labor market has shifted from low-wage manufacturing to technology-driven industries. As a result: Wages in urban areas have risen by 8% annually, improving living standards.

Minimum wages vary, with cities like Shanghai paying 2,590 yuan per month, while rural areas have significantly lower wages.

Income inequality persists, as rural workers earn less than urban counterparts.

Automation and AI are replacing low-skill jobs, creating a demand for highly skilled professionals in finance, tech, and engineering.

SIX

UNIT 4 GOVERNMENT AND THE MACRO ECONOMIC OBJECTIVE

LEARNING OBJECTIVES

LO1: the role of government Locally, nationally and internationally.

LO2: the macroeconomic aims of government- Economic growth, full employment/low unemployment, stable prices/low inflation, balance of payments stability, redistribution of income. Reasons behind the choice of aims and the criteria that governments set for each aim. possible conflicts between macroeconomic aims- Possible conflicts between aims: full employment versus stable prices; economic growth versus balance of payments stability; and full employment versus balance of payments stability.

LO3: government budget, reasons for government spending, The main areas of government spending and the reasons forand effects of spending in these areas. reasons for taxation, Taxation as the main source of government revenue and thereasons for levying taxation. classification of taxes, Examples of the different classifications of tax; progressive, regressive, proportional; and direct, indirect. The qualities of a good tax. The impact of taxation on consumers, producers, government and economy as a whole.

LO4 FISCAL POLICY- definition of fiscal policy , fiscal policy measures, The tax and spending changes, in the form of fiscal policy, that cause budget balance or imbalance. Including calculations of the size of a budget deficit or surplus.effects of fiscal policy on government macroeconomic aims. How fiscal policy measures may enable the government to achieve its macroeconomic aims.

Note: aggregate demand and aggregate supply are not required.

LO5 MONETARY POLICY- definition of money supply and monetary policy, monetary policy measures, Changes in interest rates, money supply and foreign exchange rates. effects of monetary policy on government macroeconomic aims. effects of monetary policy on government macroeconomic aims. How monetary policy measures may enable the government to achieve its macroeconomic aims.

LO6: SUPPLY SIDE POLICIES- definition of supply-side policy. supply-side policy measures . Possible supply- side policy measures include education and training, labour market reforms, lower direct taxes, deregulation, improving incentives to work and invest, and privatisation. effects of supply-side policy measures on government macroeconomic aims

LO7: ECONOMIC GROWTH- definition of economic growth, measurement of economic growth. Real Gross Domestic Product (GDP) and how it can be used to measure economic growth. GDP per head (capita). causes and consequences of recession. Meaning of recession and how a recession moves the economy within its PPC.

TERMS TO REMEMBER

1. **Fiscal Policy:** Government spending and taxation policies.
2. **Government Budget:** A financial plan outlining government revenues and expenditures.
3. **Taxation:** Compulsory payments to the government.
4. **Direct Taxes:** Taxes on income and wealth (e.g., income tax).
5. **Indirect Taxes:** Taxes on goods and services (e.g., sales tax).
6. **Economic Growth:** An increase in a country's output of goods and services.
7. **Full Employment:** A situation where all willing workers can find jobs.
8. **Inflation:** A sustained increase in the general price level.
9. **Deflation:** A sustained decrease in the general price level.
10. **GDP (Gross Domestic Product):** The total value of goods and services produced within a country.

STRUCTURED QUESTIONS

1. What are the macroeconomic aims of government?[4]

Governments aim to achieve several macroeconomic objectives to ensure economic stability and growth. One of the primary aims is economic growth, which refers to an increase in a country's Gross Domestic Product (GDP) over time. Higher economic growth leads to improved living standards, increased employment opportunities, and better public services. Another key objective is low unemployment, as high levels of joblessness can lead to lower income levels, reduced consumer spending, and increased government expenditure on welfare benefits. Governments also aim forprice stability, which involves keeping inflation at a moderate level. High inflation erodes purchasing power, whiledeflation discourages investment and spending. Additionally, maintaining a stable balance of payments is essential to avoid excessive trade deficits, which can lead to high foreign debt. Equitable income distribution is also a macroeconomic aim, as extreme income inequality can lead to social unrest and reduced economic efficiency. Finally,environmental sustainability is increasingly important, as economic activities must not compromise futuregenerations' ability to meet their needs. Governments must balance these aims carefully, as achieving one may come at the expense of another.

1. Explain the possible conflicts between macroeconomic aims.[4]

Macroeconomic objectives often conflict with each other, making it difficult for governments to achieve all goals simultaneously. For instance, economic growth and low inflation can be at odds with each other. When an economy grows rapidly, demand for goods and services increases, leading to inflationary pressures. To control inflation, the government may raise interest rates, but this, in turn, can slow down economic growth. Similarly, the goal of full employment may conflict with price stability. When more people are employed, their income rises, leading to higher consumer spending, which can push up prices. Another major conflict arises between economic growth and environmental sustainability. Industrial expansion and infrastructure development may boost GDP, but they can also lead to pollution and resource depletion. Likewise, maintaining a favourable balance of payments may contradicteconomic growth objectives. A growing economy tends to import more goods, leading to trade deficits. Governments must make trade-offs and implement balanced policies to manage these conflicts effectively.

2. State two reasons for government spending.[2]

Government spending is crucial for economic and social stability. One of the key reasons governments allocate funds is to provide public goods and services. Another important reason for government spending is income redistribution. Through social welfare programs, pensions, unemployment benefits, and subsidies, governments support low-incomegroups and reduce economic inequality. This spending helps in maintaining social stability and ensures that economic growth benefits all sections of society.

3. Why do governments impose taxes?[4]

Governments impose taxes for several economic and social reasons. One of the primary purposes is to generate revenuefor funding public services such as healthcare, education, and defense. Without taxation, governments wouldstruggle to finance essential infrastructure projects like roads, bridges, and public transport systems. Another key reasonis to control inflation. By increasing taxes on income or goods, governments reduce disposable income and consumer spending, which helps in curbing excessive demand that drives inflation. Additionally, taxation is used to redistribute wealth and reduce income inequality. Progressive taxation ensures that higher earners pay a larger proportion of theirincome in taxes, which can then be used to support lower-income groups through welfare programs. Taxes are alsoimposed to discourage the consumption of harmful goods such as cigarettes, alcohol, and sugary drinks, thereby promoting public health. Environmental taxes, such as carbon taxes, are designed to reduce pollution and encourage sustainable practices.

4. Evaluate direct taxes are better than indirect taxes.[8]

Direct and indirect taxes play essential roles in government revenue, but their effectiveness depends on various economic and social factors.

One of the main advantages of direct taxes (such as income tax and corporate tax) is that they are progressive, meaning higher-income individuals pay a larger proportion of their earnings. This helps reduce income inequality and ensures that those who can afford to pay more contribute more to public services. Additionally, direct taxes provide a stable and predictable source of government revenue, as they are collected regularly from salaries and profits.

However, direct taxes can also have drawbacks. They may discourage productivity and investment, as high-income taxrates can reduce the incentive to work harder or expand businesses. Some individuals and corporations may also engagein tax evasion by underreporting income or shifting profits to low-tax countries, reducing the government's revenue.

On the other hand, indirect taxes (such as sales tax, VAT, and excise duty) are easier to collect and harder to evade, asthey are included in the price of goods and services. They also help generate revenue from all sections of society, including those who do not earn an income, ensuring that everyone contributes to public finances.

However, indirect taxes are often regressive, meaning they place a heavier burden on lower-income individuals. Since everyone pays the same tax rate on goods and services, poorer individuals spend a larger proportion of their income onthese taxes compared to wealthier individuals. Additionally, high indirect taxes can increase the cost of living, reducing overall consumer spending and potentially slowing economic growth.

Conclusion

Direct taxes are often better for income distribution and provide a steady government revenue, but they can discourage work and investment. Indirect taxes are easier to collect and ensure widespread contribution but may disproportionately affect lower-income groups. A balanced tax system that combines both types while minimizing their drawbacks is usually the most effective approach for economic stability and social fairness.

(8 marks: 2 marks for advantages of direct taxes, 2 marks for disadvantages, 2 marks for evaluation of indirect taxes, and 2 marks for a well-structured conclusion.)

5. State the principles of taxation.[4]

The principles of taxation ensure that tax systems are fair, efficient, and effective. One fundamental principle isequity, which means that taxation should be fair and based on the ability to pay. Progressive taxation ensures that wealthier individuals contribute more. Efficiency is another key principle; the tax system should collect revenue without imposing excessive costs on the government or taxpayers. Certainty ensures that taxpayers know how much they owe, preventing confusion and disputes. Convenience is also important, meaning taxes should be easy to pay and collect, reducing administrative burdens.

6. Explain the impact of taxation.[6]

Taxation has significant economic and social effects on individuals, businesses, and government operations.

Government Revenue – Taxes are the primary source of income for the government, funding essential public services such as healthcare, education, infrastructure, and defence. Without sufficient tax revenue, governments may struggle to provide these services effectively.

Example: Income tax and corporate tax help finance public schools and hospitals.

Redistribution of Income – Progressive taxation helps reduce income inequality by ensuring that higher earners contribute more to government revenue, which can be used to support lower-income groups through welfare programs and subsidies.

Example: Higher tax rates on the wealthy can fund unemployment benefits and social security.

Influence on Consumer and Business Behavior – Taxes can impact spending, saving, and investment decisions. Higherincome taxes may reduce disposable income, lowering consumer spending. Similarly, high corporate taxes candiscourage business expansion and investment. Conversely, tax incentives can encourage investment in certain industries.

Example: Higher fuel taxes may discourage car use and promote public transportation. Conclusion

Taxation plays a crucial role in financing government activities, reducing income inequality, and shaping economic behavior. However, excessive taxation can discourage work, investment, and consumption, potentially slowing economic growth. A well-balanced tax system ensures both revenue generation and economic stability.

(6 marks: 2 marks for government revenue, 2 marks for income redistribution, and 2 marks for influence on economic behavior, with examples.)

7. Explain the effect of having a high number of firms on price, quality, choice, and profit.[6]

When an industry has many firms, competition increases, which affects price, quality, consumer choice, and profit in several ways.

Price – A high number of firms leads to intense competition, forcing businesses to lower their prices to attract customers. Consumers benefit from more affordable goods and services. However, excessive price competition can reduce profitability for firms.

Example: In the airline industry, many competing airlines result in lower ticket prices.

Quality – To stand out in a crowded market, firms focus on improving the quality of their products and services. Thisbenefits consumers as they receive better products. However, if price competition is too intense, firms may cut costs and compromise on quality.

Example: Smartphone companies constantly improve features to attract buyers.

Choice – With many firms in the market, consumers have access to a wide variety of products and services. This diversity allows people to find products that suit their preferences and budget.

Example: The fast-food industry offers multiple brands, each with different menu options.

Profit – Increased competition generally reduces profit margins, as firms must lower prices and invest in better quality to remain competitive. Smaller firms may struggle to survive, while only the most efficient businesses maintain strong profits.

Example: In the retail sector, many stores compete on price and promotions, reducing overall profits.

Conclusion: A high number of firms benefits consumers by lowering prices, improving quality, and increasing choice. However, it can also lead to lower profits for businesses, making survival difficult for smaller firms. Balancing competition with profitability is key to a healthy market.

(6 marks: 1.5 marks for each factor—price, quality, choice, and profit—with explanations and examples.)

8. Explain the effects of fiscal policy on government macroeconomic aims.[6]

Fiscal policy, which involves government taxation and spending, plays a crucial role in achieving key macroeconomic objectives such as economic growth, price stability, full employment, and a balanced budget.

Economic Growth – Expansionary fiscal policy, which includes increased government spending and tax cuts, stimulates demand and encourages business investment, leading to higher economic growth. Conversely, contractionary fiscal policy, involving higher taxes and reduced government spending, slows growth to prevent overheating.

Example: During a recession, increased government spending on infrastructure projects creates jobs and boosts economic activity.

Price Stability (Controlling Inflation) – Fiscal policy can help control inflation by adjusting government spending and taxation. Reducing government spending and increasing taxes lowers aggregate demand, helping to control inflation. However, excessive government spending can contribute to rising prices.
Example: If inflation is high, a government may increase taxes to reduce consumer spending and slow price rises.

Employment Levels – Expansionary fiscal policy creates job opportunities by boosting demand for goods and services. Higher public spending on infrastructure, healthcare, and education can directly generate employment. On the other hand, tax increases and spending cuts may lead to job losses.

Example: A government investing in public transportation projects hires more workers, reducing unemployment. Conclusion

Fiscal policy is a vital tool for achieving macroeconomic goals. While expansionary policies boost growth and employment, they may also lead to inflation. Contractionary policies help control inflation but can slow growth and increase unemployment. A balanced approach is necessary to achieve sustainable economic stability.

(6 marks: 2 marks for economic growth, 2 marks for price stability, and 2 marks for employment, with explanations and examples.)

9. Evaluate monetary policy as method to achieve macroeconomic aims of the government. [8]

Monetary policy, controlled by a country's central bank, involves adjusting interest rates, money supply, and credit availability to achieve key macroeconomic goals, such as economic growth, price stability, full employment, and balance of payments stability. While it is a powerful tool, its effectiveness depends on various factors.

One of the main advantages of monetary policy is its ability to control inflation effectively. By increasing interest rates, borrowing becomes more expensive, reducing consumer spending and business investment, which helps in lowering inflation. Conversely, during deflationary periods, lowering interest rates makes borrowing cheaper, encouraging spending and investment.

Example: The U.S. Federal Reserve raised interest rates in 2022 to combat rising inflation.

Another benefit is its flexibility and speed in responding to economic changes. Unlike fiscal policy, which requires government approval and can take time to implement, monetary policy decisions can be made quickly by the central bank to address economic issues.

However, monetary policy has limitations. One of the major drawbacks is its effectiveness in recessionary conditions.During a severe economic downturn, even if interest rates are lowered, businesses and consumers may still hesitate to borrow and spend due to low confidence. This limits the ability of monetary policy to stimulate growth.

Example: In Japan, despite low interest rates for years, economic growth remained sluggish.

Another issue is income inequality. Higher interest rates can disproportionately affect low-income individuals by making borrowing more expensive, while wealthier individuals with savings benefit from higher returns. Additionally, monetary policy may not directly address structural economic issues such as unemployment caused by automation or globalization.

Conclusion

Monetary policy is a crucial tool for achieving macroeconomic stability, particularly in controlling inflation and managing economic cycles. However, it is not always effective in boosting growth during deep recessions and may contribute to income inequality. To maximize its effectiveness, monetary policy should be used alongside fiscal policies to ensure balanced economic growth and stability.

(8 marks: 2 marks for inflation control, 2 marks for flexibility, 2 marks for limitations, and 2 marks for a balancedconclusion.)

10. Evaluate contractionary fiscal policy to control inflation [8]

Contractionary fiscal policy is a government strategy used to reduce inflation by decreasing public spending and increasing taxes. While it can be an effective tool for controlling rising prices, it also has certain limitations and negative side effects.

One of the main advantages of contractionary fiscal policy is its ability to reduce aggregate demand, which helps control inflation. By cutting government spending, there is less money circulating in the economy, which lowers consumer and business demand. Higher taxes also reduce disposable income, discouraging excessive spending and investment, leading to lower inflation.

Example: In the 1980s, the U.S. government used contractionary fiscal policies, such as reducing spending and increasing taxes, to curb high inflation.

Another benefit is that it helps maintain long-term economic stability by preventing an overheated economy. High inflation erodes the value of money, reducing purchasing power. By using contractionary fiscal policy, governments can keep inflation at a manageable level, ensuring price stability for businesses and consumers.

However, there are several disadvantages to this policy. One major issue is the risk of economic slowdown and unemployment. Reducing government spending may lead to job losses, especially in public-sector jobs and infrastructure projects. Higher taxes can also discourage business expansion, reducing investment and productivity. *Example:* In the European debt crisis (2010-2015), contractionary fiscal policies led to high unemployment in countries like Greece and Spain.

Additionally, contractionary fiscal policy may worsen income inequality, as lower-income individuals are more affected by higher taxes and reduced government spending on social programs. If spending cuts affect healthcare, education, or welfare programs, vulnerable populations may suffer the most.

Conclusion: Contractionary fiscal policy is an effective tool for controlling inflation by reducing demand, ensuring price stability, and maintaining long-term economic balance. However, it can also lead to economic slowdown, higher unemployment, and greater income inequality. Therefore, governments should implement contractionary policies cautiously, balancing inflation control with economic growth and social stability.

(8 marks: 2 marks for demand reduction, 2 marks for long-term stability, 2 marks for negative effects, and 2 marks for a balanced conclusion.)

11. Evaluate monetary policy to control inflation. [8]

Monetary policy, implemented by a country's central bank, is a key tool for controlling inflation. It primarily involves adjusting interest rates, regulating the money supply, and managing credit availability. While it can be effective in reducing inflation, it also has certain drawbacks.

One of the main advantages of monetary policy is its effectiveness in reducing demand-pull inflation, which occurs when excessive demand drives up prices. By increasing interest rates, borrowing becomes more expensive, discouraging consumer spending and business investment. This helps slow down the economy and reduce inflationary pressures.

Example: In 2022, the U.S. Federal Reserve raised interest rates to combat rising inflation, successfully slowing price increases.

Another benefit is that monetary policy can be implemented quickly and adjusted flexibly. Unlike fiscal policy, which requires government approval and may take time to implement, central banks can change interest rates or adjust the money supply promptly to respond to inflationary trends.

However, there are several disadvantages to using monetary policy for inflation control. One major issue is the risk of economic slowdown and unemployment. Higher interest rates can reduce business expansion and lead to job losses, which can slow economic growth.

Example: The European Central Bank's strict monetary policies in the early 2010s contributed to weak economic recovery and rising unemployment in some Eurozone countries.

Another limitation is that monetary policy may not be effective in controlling cost-push inflation, which is caused by rising production costs (e.g., oil price increases or supply chain disruptions). Even if interest rates are raised, inflation may persist if external factors continue to drive up costs.

Conclusion

Monetary policy is an important tool for controlling inflation, particularly demand-driven inflation, due to its flexibility and effectiveness in reducing spending. However, it has limitations, such as the risk of economic slowdown and ineffectiveness against cost-push inflation. To achieve stable inflation control, monetary policy should be used alongside fiscal measures for a balanced economic approach.

(8 marks: 2 marks for demand reduction, 2 marks for flexibility, 2 marks for negative effects, and 2 marks for a balanced conclusion.)

12. Explain the effects of supply-side policy measures on government macroeconomic aims.[6]

Supply-side policies aim to improve the productive capacity and efficiency of the economy, influencing key macroeconomic objectives such as economic growth, employment, price stability, and international competitiveness.

Economic Growth – Supply-side policies, such as investment in education, infrastructure, and research, enhance productivity and efficiency, leading to long-term economic growth. By reducing barriers to production and improving innovation, firms can expand and contribute to higher GDP.

Example: The UK government's investment in STEM education aims to create a more skilled workforce, boosting productivity.

Employment Levels – Policies such as labour market reforms, reducing unemployment benefits, and providing job training can increase workforce participation and reduce structural unemployment. Lower income taxes can also encourage more people to work.

Example: Germany's labour market reforms in the early 2000s helped reduce long-term unemployment.

Price Stability (Inflation Control) – By increasing productivity and competition, supply-side policies help control inflation in the long run. When firms operate more efficiently, production costs decrease, leading to stable or lowerprices.

Example: Deregulation in industries like telecommunications has led to lower prices and better services due to increased competition.

Conclusion

Supply-side policies play a crucial role in achieving macroeconomic stability by fostering long-term growth, reducing unemployment, and controlling inflation. However, their impact takes time to materialize, and their effectiveness depends on how well they are implemented alongside demand-side policies.

(6 marks: 2 marks for economic growth, 2 marks for employment, 2 marks for price stability, with explanations and examples.)

13. Evaluate supply-side policy measures to achieve government macroeconomic aims.[8]

Supply-side policies aim to improve the efficiency and productivity of an economy by enhancing factors such as laborskills, infrastructure, and market competition. While these policies contribute to long-term economic growth, employment, and price stability, they also have certain drawbacks.

One of the main advantages of supply-side policies is their ability to boost long-term economic growth by increasing productivity and innovation. Policies such as investment in education, training, and infrastructure help improve workforce skills and business efficiency, leading to sustained growth.

Example: Singapore's investment in education and technology has helped it become a global financial hub.

Another key benefit is reducing unemployment by making labor markets more flexible. Measures such as reducing minimum wages, improving job training, and lowering unemployment benefits encourage people to enter the workforce, reducing structural unemployment.

Example: Germany's labor market reforms in the early 2000s helped reduce long-term unemployment and boost productivity.

Additionally, supply-side policies can help control inflation by increasing competition and efficiency, which lowers production costs and improves price stability. Deregulation and privatization encourage firms to become more competitive, leading to lower prices.

Example: Deregulation in industries such as telecommunications has led to lower consumer prices and better services.

However, supply-side policies also have disadvantages. One major issue is that they take a long time to show results. Unlike demand-side policies, which have an immediate effect, investments in education, healthcare, and infrastructure take years to improve economic performance.

Another drawback is that some supply-side policies, such as reducing government spending or weakening labor protections, can increase income inequality and lead to job insecurity. Cutting taxes for businesses may boost investment but can also reduce government revenue for social welfare programs.

Example: Reducing trade union power can improve labor flexibility but may also lead to lower wages and job instability for workers.

Conclusion

Supply-side policies are crucial for long-term economic stability, as they promote growth, reduce unemployment, and help control inflation. However, they take time to be effective and may have negative social impacts, such as increased inequality. For the best results, they should be combined with demand-side policies to ensure balanced economic growth.

(8 marks: 2 marks for economic growth, 2 marks for employment, 2 marks for inflation control, and 2 marks for a balanced conclusion.)

13. Discuss the causes and consequences of a recession.[8]

A recession is a period of significant decline in economic activity across the economy, lasting for an extended period, typically defined as two consecutive quarters of negative GDP growth. Recessions can have widespread economic, social, and political consequences, affecting nearly every aspect of life within an economy. Understanding the causes of recessions and their far-reaching consequences helps policymakers and businesses to prepare and mitigate the impact.

Causes of a Recession

Several factors can lead to a recession, often acting in combination. These causes can generally be categorized as demand-side or supply-side factors, but often external shocks play a significant role as well.

Decline in Consumer and Business Confidence

One of the primary causes of a recession is a fall in both consumer and business confidence. When consumers feel uncertain about their economic future, they tend to cut back on spending. Likewise, businesses, worried about declining demand, reduce investment in new projects and may delay hiring or expansion plans. This lack of confidence leads to reduced aggregate demand, which in turn causes a contraction in economic activity.

High Interest Rates

High interest rates, often set by central banks to control inflation, can also be a significant cause of a recession. When interest rates rise, borrowing becomes more expensive for both businesses and consumers. As a result, businesses are less likely to invest in expansion or new projects, while consumers may cut back on spending, especially on big-ticket items such as homes, cars, and durable goods. Reduced demand from both consumers and businesses can cause the economy to shrink, potentially leading to a recession.

External Shocks

External factors, such as global financial crises, trade wars, or supply chain disruptions, can also trigger recessions. For example, the 2008 global financial crisis began as a banking crisis in the U.S. but quickly spread to other economies,causing widespread economic slowdowns. Similarly, disruptions in global supply chains, such as those seen during the COVID-19 pandemic, can cause shortages of goods, drive up prices, and reduce the ability of businesses to operate efficiently, leading to lower economic growth.

Decreased Investment and Innovation

Recessions can be triggered or exacerbated by a decline in business investment and innovation. When economic conditions are uncertain, businesses tend to cut back on capital expenditure and research and development (R&D) initiatives. This reduction in investment stifles productivity growth and innovation, leading to further economic contraction.

Government Austerity

In some cases, governments, to reduce public debt, may adopt austerity measures that involve cutting public spendingand increasing taxes. While these measures can improve long-term fiscal health, they can also exacerbate a recession in the short term by reducing demand and increasing the financial burden on households.

Consequences of a Recession

The consequences of a recession can be severe and wide-ranging, affecting individuals, businesses, and the economy. These effects can be felt both in the short term and the long term.

Rising Unemployment

One of the most immediate and visible effects of a recession is the rise in unemployment. As businesses face reduced demand and profitability, many resort to layoffs or hiring freezes to cut costs. Unemployment increases as workers in vulnerable sectors or industries (such as construction, manufacturing, or retail) lose their jobs. High unemployment can have a cascade effect, as reduced household incomes lower consumption, which further depresses demand in the economy.

Declining Consumer and Business Spending

During a recession, both consumer spending and business investment decline sharply. Consumers, feeling insecure about their financial situation, save more and spend less, particularly on discretionary items. Similarly, businesses, facing lower demand for goods and services, may scale back investments in new projects, reduce inventory, and delay expansion plans. This reduction in spending creates a negative feedback loop, where lower demand leads to further reductions in production and employment.

Government Budget Deficits

Recessions often result in budget deficits for governments. As the economy shrinks, government tax revenues decline because both individuals and businesses are earning less. Simultaneously, governments often increase spending on social welfare programs, such as unemployment benefits, food assistance, and other forms of financial support to help those affected by the downturn. The combination of reduced revenues and increased expenditures can lead to widening fiscal deficits, which, if sustained, may raise concerns about the long-term sustainability of government debt.

Bankruptcies and Financial Instability

Severe recessions can lead to widespread bankruptcies, particularly among small businesses that are unable to weather periods of low demand or high debt. Large corporations, particularly in industries like finance, manufacturing, andretail, may also face insolvency if they cannot adjust to changing market conditions. The failure of large businessescan cause significant disruptions in financial markets and supply chains, leading to a broader financial instability that prolongs the recession and makes recovery more difficult.

Deflation or Stagnation

In some recessions, particularly those that involve a prolonged decrease in demand, the economy may experience deflation—a general decline in prices. While this may sound like a positive development, deflation can lead to a vicious cycle where falling prices lead consumers to delay purchases, anticipating that prices will fall further. Thisworsens demand and leads to even lower prices, which can result in long-term stagnation. On the other hand, a stagflation scenario, where inflation remains high despite a recession, can complicate economic policy responses and make recovery more difficult.

Social and Psychological Effects

Recessions can have significant social consequences, especially in communities where unemployment is particularly high. Increased poverty, inequality, and stress on social safety nets can lead to social unrest, a rise in crime rates, andmental health challenges. Individuals who lose their jobs may also experience a loss of self-worth and dignity, which can lead to broader societal consequences, including a decline in social cohesion.

Conclusion

In conclusion, recessions are caused by a variety of factors, including a fall in consumer and business confidence, high interest rates, external economic shocks, and reduced investment. The consequences of a recession are far- reaching,including rising unemployment, reduced spending, budget deficits, bankruptcies, and financial instability. While recessions are a natural part of the economic cycle, their impact can be devastating. Therefore, governments often implement counter-cyclical policies, such as fiscal stimulus and monetary easing, to mitigate the effects and speed uprecovery. However, the effectiveness of these measures depends on the depth of the recession, the timing of the policy responses, and the broader global economic environment.

14. Explain the causes of economic growth.[6]

Economic growth refers to an increase in a country's output of goods and services over time, measured by the rise in real GDP. Several factors contribute to economic growth, including investment, labour force expansion, and technological advancements.

Investment in Capital Goods – Higher investment in infrastructure, machinery, and technology boosts productivity and output. Improved capital stock allows businesses to produce more efficiently, leading to sustained economic growth.

Example: China's heavy investment in manufacturing and infrastructure has contributed to rapid economic expansion.

Increase in Labor Force – A growing and skilled workforce leads to higher production levels and economic expansion. Factors such as population growth, immigration, and better education contribute to a more productive labor force.

Example: The U.S. economy benefited from an influx of skilled immigrants, driving innovation and business growth.

Technological Advancements – Innovations in production methods, automation, and digitalization improve efficiency and output. Technological progress allows businesses to lower costs and expand their production capacity.

Example: The Industrial Revolution and advancements in AI have significantly increased global productivity and economic growth.

Conclusion: Economic growth is driven by multiple factors, including investment, labour expansion, and technology. Governments and businesses play a crucial role in fostering growth through policies that support infrastructure,education, and innovation.*(6 marks: 2 marks for investment, 2 marks for labour force, and 2 marks for technology, with explanations and examples.)*

15. Explain the consequences of economic growth.[6]

Economic growth, measured by an increase in real GDP, has both positive and negative effects on an economy. While it leads to higher living standards and job creation, it can also cause inflation, income inequality, and environmental issues.

Higher Living Standards – Economic growth increases income levels, allowing people to afford better healthcare, education, and goods and services. As a result, poverty decreases, and overall well-being improves. *Example:* Rapid economic growth in South Korea transformed it from a developing to a high-income country, improving living conditions.

Job Creation and Lower Unemployment – As businesses expand due to economic growth, they require more workers, reducing unemployment and increasing job opportunities.

Example: The economic boom in the U.S. after World War II led to significant job creation and rising wages.

Inflation and Income Inequality – While growth increases wealth, it can also lead to rising prices (inflation) and widenthe income gap if wealth is not evenly distributed. High demand for goods and services may push prices up, making it harder for low-income groups to afford necessities.

Example: In India, economic growth has increased wealth, but income inequality remains a challenge.

Environmental Degradation – Rapid industrialization and economic expansion can lead to pollution, deforestation, and resource depletion, harming the environment.

Example: China's economic growth has led to severe air pollution in major cities due to industrial emissions.Conclusion

Economic growth brings significant benefits, such as higher incomes and job creation, but it also poses challenges, including inflation, inequality, and environmental concerns. Governments must balance growth with policies that ensure sustainable development and fair wealth distribution.*(6 marks: 2 marks for living standards and jobs, 2 marks for inflation and inequality, and 2 marks for environmental effects, with explanations and examples.)*

16. Explain the policies to promote economic growth.[6]

Governments implement various policies to encourage economic growth by improving productivity, investment, and overall economic efficiency. These policies can be broadly categorized into supply-side, fiscal, and monetary policies.

Supply-Side Policies – These focus on increasing the productive capacity of the economy by improving efficiency and innovation. Measures include investment in education and skills training, infrastructure development, and reducing business regulations to encourage entrepreneurship.

Example: Germany's investment in vocational training has helped improve workforce skills, boosting economic growth.

Fiscal Policy (Government Spending and Taxation) – Governments can increase public spending on infrastructure, healthcare, and education to stimulate economic activity. Lowering corporate and income taxes can also encourage investment and consumer spending.

Example: The U.S. government's tax cuts and infrastructure spending helped boost economic growth in the early 2000s.

Monetary Policy (Interest Rates and Money Supply) – Central banks can lower interest rates to make borrowing cheaper, encouraging businesses to invest and consumers to spend. Increasing the money supply can also stimulate economic activity.

Example: The European Central Bank used low interest rates after the 2008 financial crisis to support economic recovery.

Conclusion

Governments use a combination of supply-side, fiscal, and monetary policies to promote economic growth. While these policies help increase productivity, investment, and employment, they must be carefully managed to avoid inflation or excessive government debt.

(6 marks: 2 marks for supply-side policies, 2 marks for fiscal policy, and 2 marks for monetary policy, with explanations and examples.)

17. Explain the causes of unemployment.[6]

Unemployment occurs when people who are willing and able to work cannot find jobs. Several factors contribute to unemployment, including economic conditions, structural changes, and labor market inefficiencies.

Cyclical Unemployment (Demand Deficiency) – This occurs during economic recessions when businesses cut jobs due to low consumer demand. When the economy contracts, firms reduce production, leading to job losses.

Example: During the 2008 global financial crisis, many companies laid off workers, increasing unemployment rates worldwide.

Structural Unemployment – This happens when workers' skills do not match available jobs due to technological advancements, automation, or industry decline. It often requires retraining or relocation to find new employment. *Example:* The rise of automation in manufacturing has reduced demand for factory workers, leading to long-term unemployment in some regions.

Frictional Unemployment – This is temporary unemployment that occurs when workers are between jobs or enteringthe workforce. It is a natural part of a dynamic economy as people transition between roles. *Example:* A recent graduate searching for their first job experiences frictional unemployment.

Conclusion

Unemployment can result from economic downturns, skill mismatches, and job transitions. Governments can addressthese issues through policies such as education programs, job training, and economic stimulus measures to reduce joblessness and promote stable employment.

(6 marks: 2 marks for cyclical unemployment, 2 marks for structural unemployment, and 2 marks for frictional unemployment, with explanations and examples.)

18. Evaluate the policies to reduce unemployment.[8]

Unemployment is a significant issue that governments across the world try to address using a variety of economic policies. Reducing unemployment is a central objective for many governments, as it not only improves the economic stability of a country but also contributes to social well-being. The policies aimed at reducing unemployment can generally be categorized into demand-side and supply-side policies, each with its own strengths and limitations. Theevaluation of these policies involves understanding how they work, their benefits, and the potential challenges they may pose.

Expansionary Fiscal Policies

One of the most common approaches to reduce unemployment is the use of expansionary fiscal policies. This includes increasing government spending or cutting taxes to boost demand for goods and services. When the government spends more on infrastructure projects, public services, or other sectors, it directly creates jobs and stimulates demand in the economy. Similarly, tax cuts leave individuals and businesses with more disposable income, which can encourage consumption and investment, leading to more job creation.

Benefits:

Short-term job creation: Increased government spending can directly generate jobs in construction, healthcare, education, and other sectors, especially in economies that are facing cyclical unemployment (unemployment due to downturns in the economy).

Boost to aggregate demand: Tax cuts and increased spending can stimulate economic activity by increasing demand for goods and services, encouraging businesses to hire more workers to meet the demand.

Limitations:

Budget deficit and public debt: One major downside of expansionary fiscal policy is the potential increase ingovernment debt. If governments borrow to finance their spending, it could lead to budget deficits, which may be unsustainable in the long run.

Inflationary pressures: In an economy that is already operating near full capacity, an increase in demand can result indemand-pull inflation, where rising demand causes prices to increase, eroding purchasing power and potentially creating economic instability.

Monetary Policies

Monetary policy, primarily conducted by central banks, involves managing the money supply and interest rates to influence economic activity. By lowering interest rates, central banks can make borrowing cheaper, encouraging businesses to invest in expansion and hiring, and households to increase spending. Additionally, a lower interest rate can weaken the national currency, making exports more competitive, which can lead to job creation in export- oriented sectors.

Benefits:

Encourages investment and spending: Lower interest rates can lead to increased borrowing by firms and individuals, stimulating investment and consumption. This can increase demand for goods and services, resulting in more jobs being created.

Cost-effective: Monetary policy is often quicker to implement compared to fiscal policy, as central banks can adjust interest rates relatively swiftly without the need for legislative approval.

Limitations:

Time lag: While monetary policy can have a direct impact on borrowing costs, it often takes time for businesses to adjust their investment plans and for households to respond by increasing their consumption. The effects may not be immediate.

Inflation risk: If interest rates are too low for too long, it may lead to excessive demand, causing inflation. High inflation erodes purchasing power and can reduce the overall effectiveness of monetary policy in the long term.

Limited impact in a liquidity trap: If the economy is in a liquidity trap (a situation where interest rates are already very low and further cuts have no effect on economic activity), monetary policy may be less effective in reducing unemployment.

Supply-Side Policies

Supply-side policies focus on improving the long-term productive capacity of the economy by addressing structural issues in the labour market. These include measures such as vocational training, education, and reducing barriers to employment like high taxes or rigid labour laws. Training and education programs help workers gain skills that are indemand in the job market, improving their employability. Reducing regulations and taxes can also make it easier for businesses to hire new workers.

Benefits:

Long-term effectiveness: Supply-side policies are often more effective in addressing structural unemployment (unemployment caused by changes in industries or mismatches between skills and job requirements) in the long run. They can lead to a better match between workers' skills and labour market needs, reducing the natural rate of unemployment.

Improved productivity: By focusing on education and vocational training, supply-side policies enhance the productivity of the workforce, which can result in a more competitive economy and a higher level of employment.

Encourages labour force participation: By making the labour market more flexible and reducing barriers to entry, these policies can encourage more people, including those in disadvantaged groups, to join the workforce.

Limitations:

Time lag: Supply-side policies typically take a long time to show results. For example, education and training programs take years to produce skilled workers who are ready to enter the labour market.

Cost and funding: Implementing supply-side policies, such as providing extensive vocational training or improving education, requires substantial investment, which may be difficult for governments with limited resources.

Conclusion

In conclusion, while there are a variety of policies available to reduce unemployment, the effectiveness of these measures depends on the nature of the unemployment and the specific economic context of the country.Expansionary fiscal and monetary policies are effective in reducing cyclical unemployment but carry risks such as inflation and rising debt. Supply-side policies offer long-term solutions to structural unemployment but require substantial time and investment to show results. Ultimately, the best approach to reducing unemployment may involve a combination of policies, tailored to the specific needs of the economy, with careful attention to managing their potential risks and limitations.

19. How does a recession move the economy within its PPC?[4]

During a recession, economic output declines, and resources, including labour and capital, are underutilized. This moves the economy from operating on its Production Possibility Curve (PPC) to a point inside the curve, indicating inefficient use of resources. High unemployment means labor is not being fully utilized, and businesses may operate below their production capacity. The economy can only return to its PPC when demand increases, leading to higher employment and investment.

20. How does economic growth impact PPC?[2]

Economic growth results in an outward shift of the PPC, representing an increase in an economy's productive capacity. This growth can be driven by investment in capital, technological advancements, improved education and training, and efficient resource utilization. With more resources and better technology, an economy can produce more goods and services, increasing GDP.

21. Discuss the costs and benefits of economic growth in the context of different economies.[8]

Economic growth is often regarded as a desirable outcome for nations, as it typically brings a range of benefits that improve the quality of life for citizens. However, the consequences of growth are not always positive, and the costs associated with economic expansion vary significantly depending on the stage of development of a country. The costs and benefits of economic growth should be analyzed in the context of both developing and developed economies, as their experiences of growth and the challenges they face differ.

Benefits of Economic Growth

Higher Income Levels:

One of the most significant benefits of economic growth is the increase in income levels. As the economy expands, businesses generate more revenue, leading to higher profits and wages. This typically results in higher standards of living for workers, with more disposable income available for consumption. In developing economies, the growth of sectors such as agriculture, manufacturing, and services can uplift entire populations out of poverty, reducing income disparities. For developed economies, the expansion of advanced industries, services, and technology increases the earning potential of workers across diverse sectors.

Improved Public Services:

Economic growth provides governments with increased tax revenues, which can be invested in improving public services such as healthcare, education, infrastructure, and social welfare programs. In developing economies, these improvements are crucial for enhancing the quality of life and reducing poverty. For instance, economic growth may fund new schools, hospitals, and roads, making essential services more accessible. In developed economies, growth enables the government to enhance welfare systems, invest in sustainable infrastructure, and address complex social issues, such as aging populations or urbanization.

Increased Employment Opportunities:

As economies grow, businesses require more workers, which leads to job creation. In developing nations, growth in manufacturing and agriculture creates large numbers of formal and informal sector jobs, helping to reduce unemployment and underemployment. In developed nations, growth in technology, financial services, and research and development sectors offers opportunities for skilled workers, contributing to higher wages and employment stability.

Technological Advancements:

Economic growth is often driven by technological progress, which boosts productivity and innovation. In both developing and developed economies, growth allows for increased investment in R&D (Research and Development), leading to the creation of new technologies that improve efficiency across all sectors of the economy. For instance, in developing countries, technology can modernize agricultural practices or improve healthcare outcomes, while indeveloped economies, growth can lead to breakthroughs in industries such as biotechnology, clean energy, and automation, enhancing global competitiveness.

Costs of Economic Growth

Environmental Degradation and Resource Depletion:

One of the most significant costs of economic growth, especially in developing economies, is the environmental impact. Rapid industrialization and urbanization often result in increased pollution, deforestation, and the depletion of natural resources. For example, in countries with fast-growing manufacturing sectors, such as China or India, environmental damage from industrial waste, air pollution, and climate change effects is a serious concern. Over- extraction of resources, including minerals, fossil fuels, and water, can harm ecosystems, degrade biodiversity, and contribute to global warming.

In developed economies, while environmental regulations often mitigate these effects, there may still be consequences from growth in sectors like transportation, construction, and energy consumption. The challenge in developed nationsis to decouple growth from environmental degradation by fostering sustainable growth practices, such as adopting green technologies and renewable energy sources.

Social Inequality:

While economic growth increases overall income, it does not necessarily lead to equitable distribution of wealth. In developing economies, rapid growth can widen the gap between the rich and poor, leading to social inequality. Forinstance, those who are employed in high-growth sectors (e.g., finance, technology) may experience substantial wageincreases, while those in low-skill jobs may see little benefit. This can lead to inequality of opportunity, where some segments of society are excluded from the benefits of growth.

In developed economies, economic growth can also result in inequality if the benefits are disproportionately enjoyed by the wealthy or large corporations, leaving lower-income workers behind. This has been a particular issue in countries like the United States and the United Kingdom, where wage stagnation for lower and middle-income workers has coincided with growth in the stock market and profits for large companies.

Inflationary Pressures and Rising Property Prices:

In developed economies, one of the downsides of economic growth is the potential for inflation. As demand for goods and services increases, businesses may raise prices, leading to an overall rise in the price level. This erodes the purchasing power of consumers, particularly affecting low-income groups. Housing markets can also experience rapid price increases as more people move to urban areas in search of work, making housing less affordable for middle and lower-income households.

In developing economies, where many individuals may already be living close to the poverty line, rapid growth can create price volatility in basic goods like food and energy. This can exacerbate existing hardships for vulnerable groups and contribute to social unrest.

Balancing the Costs and Benefits of Economic Growth

For both developing and developed economies, sustainable economic growth requires careful policy management. Governments must prioritize inclusive growth that benefits all segments of society, particularly the most vulnerable. Policies such as progressive taxation, social welfare programs, and investments in education and healthcare can help ensure that the benefits of growth are broadly shared. Additionally, environmental policies must be implemented to minimize the ecological impact of industrialization and to promote sustainable practices such as clean energy, waste reduction, and resource conservation.

Ultimately, while economic growth has the potential to transform societies by creating wealth, improving living standards, and fostering technological advancement, it is important to balance these benefits with social equity, environmental protection, and long-term sustainability. Only through responsible governance and comprehensive policies can the costs of growth be mitigated, ensuring that its benefits reach future generations.

22. Discuss the range of policies available to promote economic growth and their effectiveness.[8]

Economic growth is essential for improving living standards, reducing poverty, and increasing employment opportunities. Governments implement various policies to stimulate growth, including monetary policies, fiscal policies, and supply-side policies. However, the effectiveness of these policies depends on factors such as the country's economic structure, political stability, global economic conditions, and the level of development.

Expansionary Monetary Policy

Governments and central banks often use monetary policy tools to influence economic growth. One of the most common strategies is lowering interest rates, which reduces borrowing costs for businesses and consumers. Lower interest rates encourage firms to invest in capital, expand operations, and hire more workers, leading to increased production and GDP growth. Additionally, lower interest rates boost consumer spending as people are more willing to take out loans for housing, cars, and other expenditures.

However, the effectiveness of expansionary monetary policy depends on several factors. If businesses and consumerslack confidence in the economy, they may not borrow and invest even when interest rates are low. Furthermore, if interest rates are already close to zero (liquidity trap), further cuts may have little impact. In developing economies,weak financial systems may limit the transmission of lower interest rates to businesses and consumers.

Expansionary Fiscal Policy

Governments can also promote growth through fiscal policies, which involve changes in government spending and taxation. By increasing public spending on infrastructure projects, education, and healthcare, governments can createjobs, improve productivity, and stimulate demand in the economy. For example, large-scale investment intransportation networks can reduce logistical costs for businesses, making them more competitive. Additionally, tax cuts for individuals and businesses increase disposable income and encourage spending and investment.

However, the effectiveness of expansionary fiscal policy depends on the government's fiscal position. If a country already has high levels of debt, excessive spending could lead to budget deficits, increasing the burden of future repayments. In addition, fiscal policies may have time lags, meaning that the impact of increased spending or tax cuts might take months or even years to materialize. If spending is inefficient or misallocated due to corruption or poor planning, fiscal policies may fail to generate sustainable economic growth.

Supply-Side Policies

Supply-side policies focus on increasing the productive capacity of the economy by improving efficiency, productivity, and competition. These policies include:

Investment in education and training: Enhances labor skills, leading to a more productive workforce that can drive long-term growth. However, results take time to manifest, as education and skill development require years of investment.

Deregulation and privatization: Reducing government regulations and encouraging private sector participation can improve efficiency and innovation. However, excessive deregulation may lead to market failures and inequality.

Encouraging research and development (R&D): Investing in technology and innovation can lead to higher productivity and competitiveness in global markets. However, R&D requires significant funding, and benefits may take time to materialize.

Improving labor market flexibility: Policies such as reducing employment protection laws or minimum wage regulations can encourage firms to hire more workers. However, such measures may also reduce job security and increase income inequality.

The effectiveness of supply-side policies largely depends on long-term investment and institutional strength. In countries with weak governance, these policies may not be effectively implemented, reducing their impact on growth.

23. Define demand-pull and cost-push inflation.[4]

Demand-pull inflation occurs when total demand in the economy exceeds total supply, leading to higher prices. Thiscan be caused by increased consumer spending, government expenditure, or expansionary monetary policy. Cost-push inflation, on the other hand, results from rising production costs, such as higher wages or raw material prices, forcing businesses to increase prices.

24. Explain how demand and cost may lead to deflation.[6]

Deflation is a sustained decrease in the general price level of goods and services in an economy. It can be caused by a fall in demand (demand-side deflation) or a decrease in production costs (cost-side deflation).

Demand-Side Deflation – This occurs when there is a decline in aggregate demand (total demand in the economy), leading to lower prices. Factors such as reduced consumer confidence, high interest rates, or lower government spending can decrease demand for goods and services. Businesses respond by cutting prices to attract buyers, causing deflation.

Example: During the Great Depression, falling consumer spending led to widespread price declines.

Cost-Side Deflation – If production costs decrease significantly, businesses may lower prices while maintaining profitmargins. This can occur due to technological advancements, increased productivity, or lower input costs (e.g., falling wages or cheaper raw materials).

Example: Advances in automation and lower oil prices can reduce production costs, leading to lower prices across industries.

Deflation can result from weak demand, which forces businesses to lower prices, or from declining production costs,which allow firms to charge less. While cost-side deflation can benefit consumers, demand-side deflation can harm economic growth by reducing business revenues and investment.

(6 marks: 3 marks for demand-side deflation, 3 marks for cost-side deflation, with explanations and examples.)

25. Discuss are the consequences of inflation and deflation for consumers, workers, savers, lenders, firms, and the economy as a whole?[8]

Both inflation (a general rise in price levels) and deflation (a general fall in price levels) have significant effects on different economic agents, including consumers, workers, savers, lenders, firms, and the overall economy.

Effects of Inflation

Consumers – Inflation reduces purchasing power, meaning people can buy fewer goods and services with the same income. This lowers their standard of living, especially for those on fixed incomes.

Example: High inflation in Venezuela led to a sharp decline in people's ability to afford basic necessities.

Workers – If wages do not increase at the same rate as inflation, workers experience a decline in real income, reducing their ability to maintain their standard of living. However, in some cases, inflation can encourage wage growth.

Savers – Inflation erodes the value of money held in savings accounts, as interest rates may not keep up with rising prices. This discourages saving and encourages spending.

Lenders – Inflation reduces the real value of money repaid by borrowers. This means lenders receive less valuable money in the future, discouraging lending.

Firms – Businesses may face higher costs for raw materials and wages, reducing profit margins. However, firms with pricing power can pass costs onto consumers, maintaining profitability.

The Economy – High inflation creates uncertainty, reducing investment and slowing economic growth. It may also lead to demand for higher wages, causing a wage-price spiral.

Effects of Deflation

Consumers – While falling prices increase purchasing power, consumers may delay purchases in expectation of further price declines, reducing overall demand.

Workers – Deflation can lead to wage cuts and job losses as firms struggle with lower revenues.

Savers – Deflation increases the real value of savings, benefiting savers who see their purchasing power rise.

Lenders – Since money gains value over time, lenders benefit because the money repaid by borrowers has more purchasing power than when it was loaned.

Firms – Businesses face declining revenues and profits, making it difficult to invest or expand. This can lead to layoffs and lower production.

The Economy – Deflation often leads to economic slowdown or recession as businesses cut jobs, investment declines, and consumer spending contracts.

Both inflation and deflation have negative effects, but inflation is generally considered less harmful when controlled. Moderate inflation encourages spending and investment, while deflation can trigger economic stagnation.Governments and central banks aim to maintain stable inflation through monetary and fiscal policies to ensure economic stability.

(8 marks: 4 marks for inflation effects, 4 marks for deflation effects, covering different economic agents with explanations and examples.)

26. Discuss the policies to control deflation.[8]

Deflation, a persistent fall in the general price level, can lead to reduced consumer spending, lower business profits, andrising unemployment. To counteract deflation, governments and central banks use monetary, fiscal, and supply- side policies to boost demand and stabilize prices.

Monetary Policies (Increasing Money Supply and Lowering Interest Rates)

Central banks play a crucial role in combating deflation by making borrowing cheaper and increasing liquidity in the economy.

Lowering Interest Rates – When interest rates decrease, borrowing becomes more affordable, encouraging businesses to invest and consumers to spend. This boosts aggregate demand and prevents further price declines. *Example:* The U.S. Federal Reserve lowered interest rates near zero after the 2008 financial crisis to stimulate growth.

Evaluation: While effective, very low or negative interest rates can reduce bank profitability and lead to excessive borrowing.

Fiscal Policies (Increasing Government Spending and Cutting Taxes) Governments use fiscal measures to stimulate demand and economic activity.

Increased Government Spending – Investment in infrastructure, healthcare, and public services creates jobs and raises incomes, encouraging consumer spending.

Example: The U.S. government implemented stimulus packages during the COVID-19 pandemic to prevent deflation.

Evaluation: This is effective in boosting demand but may lead to higher government debt.

Tax Cuts – Reducing personal and corporate taxes increases disposable income, encouraging consumption and investment.

Example: Japan implemented tax cuts to counter deflation in the 1990s.

Evaluation: While tax cuts stimulate spending, they may reduce government revenue and limit public services.

Supply-Side Policies (Encouraging Investment and Productivity Growth)

Long-term deflation control involves improving economic efficiency and business confidence.

Encouraging Business Investment – The government can provide grants, subsidies, or tax incentives to encourage firms to expand and create jobs.

Evaluation: This is effective for long-term growth but may not provide immediate relief.

Promoting Innovation and Education – Investing in research, technology, and workforce training helps improve productivity, increasing long-term economic growth and demand.

Evaluation: While beneficial, this approach requires time before yielding significant results.

A combination of monetary, fiscal, and supply-side policies is essential to control deflation effectively. While monetary policy offers quick relief, fiscal stimulus can provide long-term economic stability. However, governments must balance these measures carefully to avoid excessive debt and financial imbalances.

(8 marks: 3 marks for monetary policy, 3 marks for fiscal policy, 2 marks for supply-side policies, with explanations and evaluations.)

27. State how unemployment is measured.[2]

Unemployment is measured using two key methods:

Claimant Count – This method counts the number of people actively seeking work and claiming unemployment benefits. It is easy to collect and updated frequently, but it excludes unemployed individuals who are not eligible for benefits, such as those who have exhausted their claims.

Labour Force Survey (LFS) – This method involves a government-conducted survey to estimate the percentage of unemployed individuals actively looking for work. It provides a broader and more accurate measure than the claimant count but can be costly and time-consuming to conduct.

Both measures have limitations, as they may not fully capture underemployment, discouraged workers, or informal sector employment.

28. Discuss the consequences of unemployment for the individual, firms, and the economy as a whole.[8]

Unemployment occurs when people who are willing and able to work cannot find jobs. It has severe consequences for individuals, businesses, and the economy as a whole, leading to lower income, reduced demand, and slower economic growth.

Consequences for Individuals

Unemployment negatively affects individuals' financial stability and well-being.

Loss of Income and Reduced Standard of Living – Without a stable income, unemployed individuals struggle to afford basic necessities, leading to lower living standards.

Example: During economic recessions, many workers face financial hardship due to prolonged unemployment. Evaluation: This may lead to increased dependence on welfare programs, straining government resources.

Psychological and Social Effects – Unemployment can cause stress, depression, and loss of self-esteem. Long-term unemployment may lead to social isolation and family problems.

Evaluation: This can reduce motivation and make it harder for individuals to re-enter the workforce.

Consequences for Firms

Businesses also suffer from high unemployment due to lower demand and economic uncertainty.

Reduced Demand for Goods and Services – Unemployed individuals have lower purchasing power, leading to decreased sales for businesses.

Example: Retail and luxury industries often experience lower revenues during economic downturns. Evaluation:Firms may cut production, leading to further job losses and a cycle of economic decline.

Larger Pool of Available Labor – High unemployment increases labor supply, allowing firms to hire workers atlower wages.

Evaluation: While this may reduce costs for businesses, it can lead to worker exploitation and lower productivity due to low morale.

Consequences for the Economy as a Whole

A high unemployment rate weakens overall economic performance.

Lower Economic Growth and Output – With fewer people working, total production (GDP) declines, reducing the economy's potential output.

Example: Countries experiencing prolonged high unemployment, such as Spain after the 2008 financial crisis, saw slow economic recovery.

Evaluation: A stagnant economy can lead to long-term structural unemployment and reduced globalcompetitiveness.

Increased Government Spending on Welfare – High unemployment forces governments to spend more on benefits and unemployment assistance, leading to budget deficits.

Evaluation: This may result in higher taxes or cuts in public services, affecting economic stability.

Unemployment has severe negative effects on individuals, businesses, and the economy. While it reduces income andliving standards for individuals, it also lowers business revenues and weakens economic growth. To minimize these consequences, governments must implement policies to stimulate job creation and economic stability.

(8 marks: 2 marks for individuals, 2 marks for firms, 2 marks for the economy, and 2 marks for evaluation and conclusion.)

29. Discuss the range of policies available to reduce unemployment and how effective they might be.[8]

Governments use a combination of demand-side and supply-side policies to reduce unemployment. The effectiveness of these policies depends on the type and cause of unemployment, as well as the overall economic conditions.

Demand-Side Policies (Boosting Aggregate Demand)

These policies aim to increase overall spending in the economy, leading to higher production and job creation.

Expansionary Fiscal Policy (Increased Government Spending and Tax Cuts)

Governments can invest in infrastructure, healthcare, and education, creating direct jobs and boosting demand. Tax cuts increase disposable income, encouraging consumer spending and business investment.

Example: The U.S. stimulus packages after the 2008 financial crisis helped reduce unemployment.
Effectiveness: Works well for cyclical unemployment but may lead to budget deficits and inflation.
Expansionary Monetary Policy (Lower Interest Rates and Quantitative Easing)

Lowering interest rates makes borrowing cheaper, encouraging businesses to invest and hire more workers. Central banks can also increase the money supply to stimulate demand.

Example: The European Central Bank's low-interest policies helped reduce unemployment in the Eurozone. Effectiveness: Effective in boosting demand but may not address structural unemployment.

Supply-Side Policies (Improving Labor Market Efficiency)

These policies focus on long-term improvements in productivity and workforce skills.

Education and Training Programs

Investing in skill development helps workers adapt to changing industries, reducing structural unemployment. Example: Germany's vocational training system helps match workers with job market needs.

Effectiveness: Effective for long-term unemployment but requires time and investment.

Reducing Labor Market Regulations

Making hiring and firing easier encourages businesses to expand their workforce. Example: The UK's flexible labor laws have helped maintain low unemployment rates. Effectiveness:Increases job opportunities but may lead to job insecurity and lower wages. **Encouraging Entrepreneurship and Business Investment**

Governments can provide tax incentives, grants, and access to credit for startups and small businesses. Example: Many governments support small businesses to boost job creation.

Effectiveness: Can create jobs, but success depends on economic conditions and business confidence.

Direct Job Creation and Public Work Schemes

Governments can create jobs directly by funding large-scale infrastructure projects and community programs. Example: The New Deal in the U.S. during the Great Depression provided millions of jobs.

Effectiveness: Provides immediate employment but is expensive and may not be sustainable long-term.

A mix of demand-side and supply-side policies is necessary to effectively reduce unemployment. While fiscal and monetary policies can provide quick relief, long-term solutions require investments in education, training, and business support. However, policymakers must balance job creation with economic stability to avoid inflation, government debt, and job insecurity. (8 marks: 4 marks for policies, 4 marks for evaluation and effectiveness.)

CASE STUDY: Government Policies and Economic Stability: The Case of Germany

Germany, the largest economy in Europe, provides a significant case study on the role of government in economic management. The country's success is attributed to effective macroeconomic policies, fiscal responsibility, and structural reforms. Despite its economic strength, Germany faces challenges such as demographic shifts, income inequality, and balancing its macroeconomic aims. Germany's government plays a crucial role at local, national, and international levels, overseeing economic policies, social welfare programs, and trade relations. The macroeconomicaims of the government include economic growth, full employment, price stability, and balance of payments stability. In 2023, Germany's GDP growth stood at 1.2%, reflecting stable but moderate expansion. The country maintains low unemployment, with a rate of 3.1%, and inflation at around 3.4%, demonstrating the effectiveness of its economic policies.

Germany's government budget prioritizes infrastructure, healthcare, and education, with significant public spending on social security programs. The country's taxation system includes progressive income tax, corporate tax, and indirecttaxes like VAT. The government follows principles of fiscal discipline, aiming for balanced budgets while supporting public services. The impact of taxation is evident in Germany's well-funded public programs and efficient redistribution of income, reducing economic disparities. Fiscal policy plays a key role in Germany's economic stability. Government spending and taxation adjustments influence growth and employment. In times of economic downturn, Germany employs stimulus measures such as tax cuts and increased public investment to sustain demand. Conversely, surplus budgets help the government manage debt and prepare for future crises. Monetary policy in Germany is coordinated by the European Central Bank (ECB), which controls money supply and interest rates. TheECB's policies, such as maintaining low interest rates, have helped Germany sustain business investments and consumer spending. However, changes in monetary policy impact inflation rates and exchange rates, influencing trade competitiveness. Supply-side policies enhance Germany's long-term economic potential. The government invests in education, vocational training, and research and development to boost productivity. Labor market reforms, such as flexible work regulations and incentives for employment, have contributed to high labor force participation. Deregulation in key industries promotes competition and efficiency, ensuring sustainable growth. Germany's economic growth is measured through real GDP and GDP per capita, indicating productivity and living standards. The country's robust manufacturing and technology sectors drive economic expansion. However, challenges such as demographic aging pose risks to future growth. With an aging population and declining birth rates, Germany faces labor shortages and increased social security costs. Policies encouraging workforce participation and skilled migration are essential to address these demographic trends.

Assessment Questions (30 Marks Total)

1. What was Germany's GDP growth rate in 2023, and what does it indicate about its economy? (1 mark)

Germany's GDP growth rate in 2023 was 2%, indicating stable but moderate economic expansion.

2. State two main sources of government revenue in Germany and their impact on public services. (2 marks)

(1) Progressive income tax funds social security programs.

(2) VAT generates revenue for infrastructure and public projects.

3. Explain the role of monetary policy in Germany's economy and its impact on inflation. (2 marks)

The European Central Bank controls monetary policy, regulating money supply and interest rates to manage inflation and economic stability.

4. Discuss two fiscal policy measures Germany has implemented to sustain economic stability. (4 marks)

(1) Public investment in infrastructure boosts economic activity.

(2) Balanced budget policies preventexcessive national debt.

5. How do Germany's supply-side policies contribute to economic growth and employment? (4 marks)

Investment in education and vocational training improves workforce skills, while deregulation fosters business efficiency and competition, increasing employment.

6. Explain the impact of Germany's taxation system on income distribution and economic efficiency. (5 marks)

Germany's progressive tax system redistributes wealth, reducing income inequality. High tax rates fund social programs, ensuring equitable access to healthcare and education. However, heavy taxation on businesses may discourage investment. Efficient tax policies, as seen in Germany, contribute to economic stability by balancing revenue collection and economic incentives.

7. How does Germany's aging population affect its economy, and what policies can address this challenge? (6 marks)

Germany's aging population presents a significant challenge, leading to a shrinking workforce and increasing pressure on social security and healthcare systems. With fewer workers contributing to tax revenues, pension funds face sustainability issues. To counter these challenges, Germany has introduced policies such as raisingthe retirement age, incentivizing higher workforce participation, and investing in automation and AI to offset labor shortages. Additionally, Germany promotes skilled migration to fill employment gaps, ensuring that key sectors remain productive. The government also focuses on family-friendly policies, including childcare support and parental benefits, to encourage higher birth rates over the long term. These combined efforts help mitigate the economic impact of an aging population and sustain growth.

8. Discuss the possible conflicts between Germany's macroeconomic aims and how the government manages these challenges. (6 marks)

Balancing Germany's macroeconomic aims presents inherent conflicts. For instance, achieving full employment may lead to inflationary pressures, as increased consumer demand drives up prices. Similarly, high economic growth can worsen the balance of payments, as rising incomes boost imports more than exports. The German government addresses these conflicts through a combination of fiscal, monetary, and supply-side policies. For example, monetary tightening by the ECB helps control inflation, while fiscal discipline ensures that government spending remains within sustainable limits. Additionally, Germany invests in technology and productivity improvements to enhance competitiveness, thereby maintaining export strength. Through these measures, Germany effectively navigates conflicts between its macroeconomic objectives while ensuring long-term stability

CASE STUDY:

A Comparative Analysis of the United States and Colombia

Economic policies shape the trajectory of national growth, influencing employment, inflation, income distribution, and global trade. Comparing the United States and Colombia provides insight into how different governmental strategies impact economic stability and development. While the U.S. is a global economic powerhouse with advanced financial institutions and technology-driven industries, Colombia, as a developing economy, faces challenges in achieving sustained growth and reducing inequality.

The U.S. government plays a pivotal role in economic management at local, national, and international levels. The macroeconomic aims of the U.S. government include achieving high economic growth, low unemployment, stable prices, and a balanced trade account. As of 2023, the U.S. reported a GDP growth rate of 2.1%, driven by consumer spending, technological innovation, and service sector expansion. Unemployment stood at 3.7%, indicating a relatively stable labor market, while inflation hovered at 3.2%, reflecting the Federal Reserve's efforts to control price stability.

In contrast, Colombia has experienced fluctuating economic conditions. In 2023, Colombia's GDP growth was 1.5%,signalling moderate progress amid external economic pressures. The country has a higher unemployment rate of 10.4%, which reflects ongoing challenges in job creation. Inflation in Colombia remained elevated at 9.3%, influenced by supply chain disruptions and currency depreciation. The Colombian government focuses on stabilizing inflation while promoting investment in infrastructure and human capital to foster long-term growth.

Government budgets and taxation systems in both nations differ significantly. The U.S. follows a mixed taxation system, combining progressive income tax, corporate tax, and indirect taxes such as sales tax. Federal and state governments allocate budgets toward social security, healthcare, education, and infrastructure. Colombia, on the otherhand, faces issues with tax compliance and informality in its labor market, which limits government revenue. Its taxsystem is also progressive, but inefficiencies lead to fiscal deficits, necessitating international loans and fiscal reforms to ensure sustainable development.

Fiscal policy plays a crucial role in economic stability for both countries. The U.S. utilizes countercyclical fiscal measures, increasing government spending during recessions and reducing expenditure during economic booms. Infrastructure development, tax incentives, and social welfare programs are key fiscal tools. Colombia, meanwhile, faces constraints due to budget deficits, requiring external financial support. The government has implemented public investment programs to stimulate growth and employment but struggles with inefficiencies in budget execution.

Monetary policy is another distinguishing factor. The U.S. Federal Reserve independently sets interest rates and controls money supply, influencing inflation and employment. Interest rate hikes in 2023 helped curb inflation but raised borrowing costs. Colombia's central bank similarly adjusts interest rates to control inflation; however, external factors such as capital flows and exchange rate volatility create challenges in maintaining monetary stability.

Supply-side policies in the U.S. emphasize innovation, deregulation, and workforce skill development. Investments inresearch and education drive technological advancements, maintaining economic competitiveness. In Colombia, supply-side measures focus on improving education access, labor market reforms, and infrastructure expansion. However, structural weaknesses, such as low productivity and informal employment, hinder rapid progress.

Economic growth, measured through real GDP and GDP per capita, indicates disparities between the two nations. The U.S. GDP per capita stands at approximately $76,000, reflecting high living standards and productivity. Conversely, Colombia's GDP per capita is around $7,500, illustrating income inequality and developmental gaps.

Challenges such as poverty, inadequate healthcare, and limited access to quality education contribute to disparities in living standards.

Assessment Questions (30 Marks Total)

1. What was the GDP growth rate of the U.S. in 2023, and what does it indicate about its economy? (1 mark)

The U.S. GDP growth rate in 2023 was 2.1%, indicating steady economic expansion driven by consumer spending and technological advancements.

2. Identify two major economic challenges faced by Colombia in 2023. (2 marks)

(1) High unemployment at 10.4%, indicating difficulties in job creation.

(2) Inflation at 9.3%, reducing purchasing power and increasing the cost of living.

3. Explain how fiscal policy is used to stabilize the economy in the U.S. (2 marks)

The U.S. government adjusts public spending and taxation to manage economic fluctuations. During downturns, it increases spending and reduces taxes to stimulate growth; during booms, it limits spending to prevent overheating.

4. Compare the monetary policies of the U.S. and Colombia. (4 marks)

The U.S. Federal Reserve sets interest rates to control inflation and employment. Colombia's central bank follows a similar strategy but faces challenges from currency depreciation and external financial pressures. While the U.S. enjoys monetary policy independence, Colombia is more susceptible to external shocks.

5. How does taxation impact economic development in Colombia compared to the U.S.? (4 marks)

The U.S. has an efficient tax collection system that funds public services, ensuring economic stability. Colombia struggles with tax compliance and informality, reducing government revenue and limiting public investment in education and healthcare. These inefficiencies contribute to income inequality and slower development.

6. Explain the impact of supply-side policies on economic growth in both countries. (5 marks) Supply-side policies in the U.S. enhance productivity through investments in education, research, and deregulation. These measures foster innovation and business expansion. In Colombia, supply-side policies aim to improve education and labor market flexibility, but challenges such as infrastructure deficits and informal employment slow progress.Effective implementation of supply-side policies in both nations determines their long- term economic stability and growth potential.

7. Discuss the impact of income distribution and social policies on living standards in the U.S. and Colombia. (6 marks)

The U.S. benefits from high income levels and well-developed social programs, reducing poverty and ensuring access to healthcare and education. However, income inequality remains a concern, with disparities in wealth distribution.

Colombia faces greater inequality, with a significant portion of its population in poverty. Limited access to quality education and healthcare hampers social mobility. While government initiatives aim to improve living standards, economic constraints and corruption limit their effectiveness. Addressing income distribution through equitable tax policies and enhanced social programs is crucial for sustainable development.

8. How do government policies in the U.S. and Colombia address economic stability, and what challenges do they face? (6 marks)

The U.S. implements a mix of fiscal and monetary policies to maintain economic stability. The Federal Reserve's interest rate adjustments and government spending policies ensure steady growth and controlled inflation. Challenges include rising public debt and trade imbalances. Colombia focuses on stabilizing inflation and promoting investment, but political instability and budget deficits hinder progress. While both countries strive for macroeconomic stability, the effectiveness of their policies depends on governance, external economic conditions, and long-term structural reforms.

SEVEN

UNIT 5: ECONOMIC DEVELOPMENT

LEARNING OBJECTIVES

LO1: indicators of living standards- Real GDP per head and the Human Development Index (HDI). The components of real GDP and HDI. The advantages and disadvantages of real GDP and HDI. comparing living standards and income distribution. Reasons for differences in living standards and income distribution within and between countries.

LO2: Difference between absolute and relative poverty. The causes of poverty including unemployment, low wages, illness and age. Policies including those promoting economic growth, improved education, more generous state benefits, progressive taxation, and national minimum wage to remove poverty.

LO3: the factors that affect population growth. Birth rate, death rate, net migration, immigration and emigration. reasonsfor different rates of population growth in different countries. How and why birth rates, death rates and net migration vary between countries. the effects of changes in the size and structure of population on different countries. The concept of an optimum population. The effects of increases and decreases in population size and changes in the age and genderdistribution of population. *Note: interpretation of a population pyramid is required, but drawing is not.*

LO4: differences in economic development between countries. Causes and impacts of differences in income; productivity; population growth; size of primary, secondary and tertiary sectors; saving and investment; education; and healthcare.

TERMS TO REMEMBER

1. **Living Standards** – A measure of the quality of life of individuals within a country, often assessed through factors such as income, access to healthcare, education, and housing conditions.

2. **Real GDP per Head** – The total output of goods and services (GDP) in an economy, adjusted for inflation, divided by the population, providing an average income per person.

3. **Human Development Index (HDI)** – A composite measure of development that considers three key factors: life expectancy (health), education levels (mean and expected years of schooling), and per capita income (standard of living).

4. **Components of Real GDP** – The four main components of real GDP include:

5. **Consumption (C):** Household spending on goods and services.

6. **Investment (I):** Business expenditures on capital goods.

7. **Government Spending (G):** Public sector expenditures on services and infrastructure.

8. **Net Exports (X-M):** The difference between exports and imports.

9. **Components of HDI** – HDI is calculated using three dimensions:

10. **Health:** Measured by life expectancy at birth.

11. **Education:** Measured by mean and expected years of schooling.

12. **Income:** Measured by Gross National Income (GNI) per capita.

13. **Income Distribution** – The way income is divided among individuals or households in an economy, often assessed through measures like the Gini coefficient.

14. **Absolute Poverty** – A condition where individuals lack basic necessities such as food, shelter, and healthcare, typically defined as living on less than $2.15 per day (as per the World Bank).

15. **Relative Poverty** – A condition where individuals have significantly lower income compared to the average in their society, limiting their ability to participate fully in economic and social activities.

16. **Unemployment** – The state of being willing and able to work but unable to find a job, typically measured as a percentage of the labor force.

17. **Low Wages** – Earnings that are insufficient to meet basic living expenses, often leading to financial hardship and economic inequality.

18. **Economic Growth** – The increase in the output of goods and services in an economy over time, measured by the rise in real GDP.

Progressive Taxation – A tax system where the tax rate increases as income levels rise, ensuring that higher earners contribute a larger proportion of their income in taxes.

19. National Minimum Wage – The legally set lowest wage that employers must pay workers, aimed at protecting low-income employees from exploitation.

20. Birth Rate – The number of live births per 1,000 people in a population per year.

21. Death Rate – The number of deaths per 1,000 people in a population per year.

22. Net Migration – The difference between the number of people entering (immigration) and leaving (emigration) a country over a given period.

23. Immigration – The process of individuals moving into a country to live and work.

24. Emigration – The process of individuals leaving their home country to settle in another.

25. Optimum Population – The ideal population size where resources are efficiently utilized to achieve the highest possible standard of living.

26. Population Size – The total number of people living in a specific geographic area, such as a country or region.

27. Age Distribution – The proportion of different age groups within a population, typically categorized into young (0-14), working-age (15-64), and elderly (65+).

28. Gender Distribution of Population – The ratio of males to females in a population, often expressed as a percentage or a ratio (e.g., 102 males per 100 females).

29. Population Pyramid – A graphical representation of a population's age and gender distribution, showing the number or percentage of people in each age group.

30. Economic Development – The process of improving economic well-being and quality of life through factors such as higher incomes, better healthcare, education, and infrastructure.

31. Income – The money received by individuals or households through wages, salaries, investments, or government benefits.

32. Productivity – The efficiency of production, measured as output per worker or output per unit of input (e.g., labor or capital).

33. Population Growth – The increase in the number of people in a region over time, influenced by birth rates, death rates, and net migration.

34. Primary Sector – The sector of the economy that involves the extraction of natural resources, such as agriculture, fishing, forestry, and mining.

35. Secondary Sector – The sector that involves manufacturing and industrial production, converting raw materials into finished goods.

36. Tertiary Sector – The service sector, including industries such as retail, healthcare, banking, education, and tourism.

37. Saving: The portion of income not spent on consumption, often deposited in banks or used for future investment.

38. Investment: The use of savings to purchase assets or capital goods that generate income or economic growth.

39. Education – A crucial factor in economic development, referring to the process of acquiring knowledge and skills that enhance productivity and employability.

40. Healthcare – The provision of medical services and public health initiatives to improve life expectancy and overall well-being in a population.

STRUCTURED QUESTIONS

1. Explain the causes of poverty. [6]

Poverty arises due to multiple factors. One significant cause is **low levels of education and skills**, which reduce employment opportunities and limit earning potential. **Unemployment** is another major factor—when individuals cannot find work, they struggle to afford necessities. **Low wages** also contribute to poverty, especially in countries where labor is abundant, and wages are not protected by minimum wage laws.

Another cause is **poor healthcare and malnutrition**, which affect productivity and limit economic mobility. **Rapid population growth** can increase poverty by straining resources and public services. Additionally, **political instabilityand corruption** often prevent economic development and proper distribution of wealth. Lastly, **external factors**, such as natural disasters or trade restrictions, can push communities into poverty by destroying livelihoods and limiting economic opportunities.

2. Discuss the policies to alleviate poverty and redistribute income. [8]

Governments use various policies to **reduce poverty and redistribute income**. One approach is **progressive taxation**, where higher-income individuals pay a larger percentage of their income in taxes, reducing income inequality. The government can then use this tax revenue to fund **welfare programs**, such as unemployment benefits, food assistance, and housing support.

Another policy is **investment in education and healthcare**, which helps improve skills and productivity, allowing individuals to secure better-paying jobs. Governments can also introduce **minimum wage laws** to ensure fair wages for workers. **Subsidized housing and healthcare** can reduce the financial burden on low-income groups, improving living standards.

In addition, **job creation programs** through infrastructure projects or government employment schemes help reduce unemployment. Finally, **microfinance initiatives** support small businesses by providing affordable credit, encouraging entrepreneurship and income generation among the poor.

3. State the components of real GDP and HDI. [4]

RealGDP (Gross Domestic Product) is composed of:

Consumption (C) – Spending by households on goods and services. Investment (I) – Business spending on capital goods and infrastructure.

Government spending (G) – Expenditures on public services, defense, and infrastructure. Net exports (X-M) – The difference between exports (X) and imports (M).

The Human Development Index (HDI) consists of three components: Health – Measured by life expectancy at birth.

Education – Measured by mean and expected years of schooling.

Standard of living – Measured by GNI (Gross National Income) per capita.

4. Explain the advantages and disadvantages of real GDP and HDI. [6]

Advantages of Real GDP:

Measures **economic performance** and allows comparison between countries. Helps governments and policymakers in **planning economic policies**.

Indicates **living standards**, as higher GDP often leads to higher incomes.

Disadvantages of Real GDP:

Does not account for **income inequality**—a high GDP does not mean wealth is evenly distributed. Excludes **non-market activities**, such as unpaid work or informal economies.

Ignores **environmental damage**, such as pollution and resource depletion.

Advantages of HDI:

Provides a broader measure of well-being by including education and health. Helps governments focus on social policies, not just economic growth.

Enables comparisons of human development across countries.

Disadvantages of HDI:

Does not consider income inequality within a country.

Ignores political and social freedoms, which also impact development. Relieson limited indicators, excluding factors like environmental quality.

5. Explain reasons for differences in living standards and income distribution within and between countries. [6]

Living standards and income distribution differ due to economic growth rates—developed nations generally have higher productivity, leading to higher wages. Education and skill levels also play a role; countries with better education systems produce a more skilled workforce, leading to higher incomes.

Within countries, urban-rural divides often result in income disparities, as urban areas typically have better infrastructure, jobs, and services. Government policies, such as taxation and welfare systems, also influence income distribution—progressive tax systems reduce inequality, whereas weak redistribution policies lead to greater income gaps.

Between countries, factors like access to resources, industrialization levels, and political stability impact income levels. Developing nations often rely on low-value primary industries, whereas developed countries have diversified economies with high-paying sectors like technology and finance.

6. Explain the factors that affect population growth. [6]

Population growth is influenced by several factors, including the birth rate, death rate, and net migration. High birth rates can be driven by cultural and religious factors, lack of contraception, and economic incentives for large families. Conversely, birth rates decline with higher education levels, particularly for women, and better access to healthcare.

Death rates are affected by healthcare quality, nutrition, and sanitation—improved medical advancements and public health measures reduce mortality. Lastly, net migration affects population size—countries with strong economiesattract immigrants, increasing population, while those with weak economies may experience emigration.

7. Explain the reasons for different rates of population growth in different countries. [6]

Different rates of population growth occur due to economic development levels—developed nations typically have lower birth rates due to better education, healthcare, and family planning. In contrast, developing countries may experience high birth rates due to cultural traditions, lack of contraception, and economic reliance on large families.

Government policies also play a role—pro-natalist policies (encouraging births) in some countries and anti-natalist policies (limiting births) in others influence growth. Additionally, immigration policies can increase population growth in developed countries by attracting skilled labor.

8. Explain the effects of changes in the size and structure of population on different countries. [6]

Changes in population size and structure affect economic growth, employment, and social services. A rapidly growing population increases demand for jobs, healthcare, and education, straining public services in developing countries. However, it can also provide a large labor force, driving economic expansion.An aging population, common indeveloped nations, leads to higher dependency ratios, increasing healthcare and pension costs. Countries with declining populations may face labor shortages and economic stagnation, requiring policies to attract immigration.

9. How and why birth rates, death rates, and net migration vary between countries. [6]

Birth rates vary due to economic, cultural, and healthcare factors—developing nations often have higher birth rates due to tradition, lack of contraception, and high infant mortality rates. Developed nations experience lower birth rates due to career priorities and urbanization.

Death rates depend on healthcare availability, living conditions, and disease prevalence. Developed nations have lowerdeath rates due to advanced medical care, whereas poorer countries struggle with high mortality due tomalnutrition and infectious diseases.Net migration varies based on economic opportunities, conflict, and quality of life. People migrate to countries with better job prospects and political stability, while war, poverty, or lack of opportunities drive emigration.

10. Discuss the effects of increases and decreases in population size and changes in the age and gender distribution of population. [8]

A population increase can provide a larger workforce, boosting economic growth. However, if job creation does notmatch growth, it can lead to unemployment, poverty, and pressure on infrastructure. A declining population may lead to labor shortages and reduced economic output.

Changes in the age structure also matter—aging populations create higher dependency ratios, increasing pension and healthcare costs. Conversely, a youthful population can boost productivity but may also require heavy investment ineducation and healthcare. Gender imbalances, often due to selective birth rates or migration patterns, can cause social and economic challenges.

11. Explain the differences in economic development between countries. [6]

Differences in economic development arise from historical, geographical, and policy factors. Developed nations have strong industrial bases, skilled workforces, and advanced technology, leading to higher incomes and better infrastructure. In contrast, developing countries may struggle with low productivity, weak governance, and unstable financial systems.

Natural resources, trade policies, and education levels also play a role—resource-rich nations can generate wealth, while education investment enhances human capital. Additionally, political stability and governance impact long- term development prospects.

CASE STUDY

Global Disparities and Policy Interventions

Economic development varies significantly across countries due to differences in living standards, income distribution, and key economic indicators. Two primary measures used to assess living standards are Real GDP per head and the Human Development Index (HDI). Real GDP per head reflects the average income per person in an economy and is widely used to compare economic performance. However, it does not account for non-economic factors such as education and healthcare. In contrast, the HDI incorporates life expectancy, education levels, and income to provide a more comprehensive measure of human development. While Real GDP per head is a useful economic indicator, it fails to capture income distribution disparities within a country. HDI, on the other hand, provides a broader perspective but may not fully reflect short-term economic fluctuations.

Differences in living standards and income distribution exist both within and between countries due to factors such as resource allocation, education access, and government policies. High-income nations tend to have better infrastructure,healthcare, and social welfare systems, leading to improved living conditions. In contrast, developing countries often struggle with income inequality, poor healthcare, and limited access to education. For example, Scandinavian countries exhibit high HDI rankings due to strong social policies, whereas sub-Saharan African nations face challenges due to political instability and low economic productivity.

Poverty is another significant challenge affecting economic development. Absolute poverty refers to a condition where individuals cannot meet basic necessities such as food, shelter, and healthcare, while relative poverty compares individuals' economic status to the average income in their society. Causes of poverty include unemployment, lowwages, illness, and age-related vulnerabilities. Countries implement various policies to reduce poverty, including promoting economic growth, improving education, increasing state benefits, enforcing progressive taxation, and implementing a national minimum wage. For instance, China's rapid economic growth has lifted millions out ofpoverty, while Scandinavian countries have used strong welfare policies to reduce income disparities.

Population growth also plays a crucial role in economic development. Birth rates, death rates, and net migration affect population dynamics, influencing labor supply and economic sustainability. Developing nations often experience highbirth rates due to limited access to contraception and cultural norms, whereas developed countries face declining birth rates due to changing lifestyle choices. Migration impacts population size, as countries with better economic opportunities attract immigrants seeking employment. For instance, Germany has benefited from skilled labor migration, while countries experiencing brain drain struggle with labor shortages.

The effects of population changes vary. A growing population can provide a larger workforce and boost economic output, but overpopulation may strain resources, leading to unemployment and poverty. Conversely, population decline can reduce economic growth due to a shrinking labor force. The concept of optimum population suggests that an ideal balance between population size and resource availability is crucial for sustainable development. Changes inage and gender distribution also influence economies, as aging populations require more healthcare and pension support, while younger populations drive productivity and innovation.

Economic development disparities between countries stem from factors such as differences in income, productivity, population growth, and sectoral composition. Nations reliant on primary industries like agriculture often face slower growth, while those with strong secondary (manufacturing) and tertiary (services) sectors experience rapid expansion.For example, Singapore's emphasis on a knowledge-based economy has driven high productivity and income levels, whereas resource-dependent economies, such as Nigeria's oil industry, face volatility. Education and healthcare investments significantly impact development, as well-trained workforces and healthy populations contribute to long-term economic growth.

Investment and savings also influence development. Countries with higher savings rates can fund infrastructure projects and technological advancements, fostering sustainable growth. Policies aimed at improving education, healthcare, and economic diversification can help bridge development gaps between nations, ensuring long-term stability and prosperity.

Assessment Questions (30 Marks Total)

1. What is the difference between Real GDP per head and the Human Development Index (HDI)? (1 mark)

Real GDP per head measures the average income per person, while HDI incorporates income, education, and life expectancy for a broader assessment of human development.

2. State two advantages and two disadvantages of using Real GDP per head as a measure of living standards. (2 marks)

Advantages:

(1) Easy to calculate and compare between countries,

(2) Provides a clear economic indicator.

Disadvantages:

(1) Does not reflect income inequality,

(2) Ignores non-economic factors like education and healthcare.

3. Explain the main causes of poverty, distinguishing between absolute and relative poverty. (2 marks)

Absolute poverty is when people lack basic needs like food and shelter, while relative poverty is when income is lower than the societal average. Causes include unemployment, low wages, lack of education, and poor health.

4. Discuss two policies a government can implement to reduce poverty and their potential effectiveness. (4 marks)

(1) Progressive taxation redistributes wealth but may discourage high earners.

(2) Improved education enhances skills and employment prospects, fostering long-term economic growth.

5. How do birth rate, death rate, and migration impact a country's economic development? (4 marks)

High birth rates increase labor supply but strain resources, while low birth rates lead to aging populations and economic slowdown. Migration can fill labor gaps or cause brain drain, affecting national productivity.

6. Evaluate the role of education and healthcare in promoting economic development. (5 marks)

Education plays a critical role in economic development by equipping individuals with necessary skills, fostering innovation, and improving productivity. Countries with high literacy rates and robust education systems, such as South Korea, have experienced rapid industrial growth. Similarly, healthcare contributes to economic progress by ensuring a healthy workforce, reducing absenteeism, and increasing life expectancy. Investments in healthcare and education create a cycle of sustained development, as seen in Scandinavian nations, where these sectors receive significant funding, leading to high standards of living and economic stability.

7. How does population growth affect economic development, and what is the concept of an optimum population? (6 marks)

Rapid population growth can provide a larger labor force, potentially boosting economic productivity. However, if resources such as education, healthcare, and job opportunities cannot keep pace, overpopulation can lead to unemployment, poverty, and strain on public services. Conversely, a declining population may result in labor shortages and economic stagnation, as seen in Japan, where an aging workforce is impacting productivity. The conceptof optimum population suggests that a country should maintain a balance between population size and resource availability to maximize economic efficiency. Countries like Singapore have strategically managed population policies to maintain economic growth and resource sustainability.

8. Discuss the impact of income inequality on economic growth and social stability. How do policies such as progressive taxation and state welfare address these issues? (6 marks)

High income inequality can hinder economic growth by reducing consumer spending, limiting access to quality education and healthcare, and increasing social unrest. Unequal societies often experience lower levels of social mobility, creating economic inefficiencies and political instability. Progressive taxation ensures wealth redistribution by imposing higher tax rates on the wealthy, funding social programs that benefit lower-income groups. State welfare policies, including unemployment benefits, healthcare subsidies, and housing assistance, provide a safety net for vulnerable populations. Countries like Sweden have successfully used these measures to create a more equitable society, fostering both economic growth and social cohesion.

CASE STUDY Economic Development and Challenges: The Case of Brazil

Brazil, the largest economy in South America, presents a compelling case study of economic development, poverty alleviation, and population dynamics. The country's growth trajectory has been shaped by factors such as industrialization, globalization, and government policies aimed at reducing economic disparities. However, challenges persist in areas like income distribution, living standards, and economic stability.

Economic indicators such as Real GDP per head and the Human Development Index (HDI) provide insights into Brazil's development. Brazil's Real GDP per head was approximately $8,570 in 2023, reflecting moderate economic growth. However, this measure does not account for income inequality, a persistent issue in Brazil, where the wealthiest 10% of the population control over 40% of national income. HDI, which considers life expectancy, education, and income, ranks Brazil 87th globally, highlighting improvements in literacy rates and healthcare but also emphasizing ongoing social disparities.

Poverty remains a significant concern in Brazil, with absolute and relative poverty affecting millions. Absolute poverty is defined by an inability to meet basic needs such as food and shelter, while relative poverty is based on income disparities within the country. The causes of poverty in Brazil include high unemployment rates (reaching 8.3% in 2023), low wages, inadequate education, and regional disparities. The government has implemented policies such as Bolsa Família, a cash transfer program benefiting over 14 million low-income families, and progressive taxation to address wealth inequality.

Population dynamics also play a crucial role in Brazil's economic development. The country has experienced a declining birth rate, from 6 children per woman in the 1960s to 1.6 in 2023, due to urbanization, increased female workforce participation, and improved access to contraception. Net migration has also influenced Brazil's economy, with an influx of skilled labor benefiting industries while emigration of skilled professionals to North America and Europe has led to concerns over brain drain. The population structure is shifting, with a growing elderly population requiring increased healthcare and pension support.

Differences in economic development across Brazil stem from factors such as income disparities, productivity, sectoral composition, and education levels. The southeast region, home to São Paulo and Rio de Janeiro, boasts strong industrial and service sectors, driving economic growth. In contrast, the northeast lags in infrastructure and jobopportunities, contributing to higher poverty rates. Investment in education and healthcare is vital for reducing these regional disparities. Brazil allocates 6% of its GDP to education, yet quality varies significantly, impacting workforce competitiveness and long-term economic growth.

Foreign investment and savings also influence Brazil's economic trajectory. As one of the world's largest agricultural exporters, Brazil benefits from global trade but remains vulnerable to commodity price fluctuations. Policies aimed at economic diversification, infrastructure investment, and innovation are crucial for sustainable growth. Efforts to reduce reliance on raw material exports and boost technology-driven industries could enhance long-term stability.

Assessment Questions (30 Marks Total)

1. What is the current ranking of Brazil on the Human Development Index (HDI), and what does this ranking indicate? (1 mark)

Brazil ranks 87th on the HDI, indicating moderate human development with improvements in literacy and healthcare but persistent social disparities.

2. State two advantages and two disadvantages of using Real GDP per head as a measure of living standards in Brazil. (2 marks)

Advantages:

(1) Provides an easy comparison of economic output,

(2) Helps measure economic growth.

Disadvantages:

(1) Does not reflect income inequality,

(2) Ignores non-monetary factors like health and education.

3. Explain the main causes of poverty in Brazil, distinguishing between absolute and relative poverty. (2 marks)

Absolute poverty refers to the lack of basic necessities, while relative poverty compares individuals to national income levels. Causes include high unemployment, low wages, inadequate education, and regional disparities.

4. Discuss two government policies implemented in Brazil to reduce poverty and their effectiveness. (4 marks)

(1) Bolsa Família provides direct financial aid to low-income families, improving child education and nutrition.

(2) Progressive taxation redistributes wealth but faces implementation challenges due to tax evasion and inefficiencies.

5. How have changes in birth rate, death rate, and migration influenced Brazil's economy? (4 marks)

Brazil's declining birth rate reduces future labor supply, while increasing life expectancy places pressure onsocial services. Migration trends have brought skilled workers into key industries but have also led to brain drain as professionals leave for better opportunities abroad.

Evaluate the impact of education and healthcare on Brazil's economic development. (5 marks) **Answer:** Education and healthcare are crucial for long-term economic growth. Brazil spends 6% of its GDP on education, yetdisparities in quality between urban and rural areas affect workforce skill levels. Improved education increases labor productivity, innovation, and competitiveness in the global market. Similarly, advancements in healthcare boost life expectancy and workforce efficiency, reducing absenteeism and increasing national productivity. Countries with better-funded education and healthcare systems, such as Germany, demonstrate the long-term benefits of investment inhuman capital. Brazil must address regional inequalities to fully leverage these sectors for economic growth.

6. How does Brazil's population structure affect its economic development, and what is the concept of an optimum population? (6 marks)

Brazil's aging population creates challenges for pension and healthcare systems, while declining birth rates may lead to labor shortages. However, a lower dependency ratio can boost economic growth if the working-age population is well-educated and employed. The concept of optimum population suggests that a country should maintain a balance between population size and resources. In Brazil, economic policies focused on education and job creation can help achieve this balance, ensuring sustainable development and improved living standards.

7. Discuss the impact of income inequality on Brazil's economic growth and social stability. How do policies like progressive taxation and state welfare address these issues? (6 marks)

High income inequality in Brazil leads to reduced consumer spending, social unrest, and economic inefficiencies. The wealth gap limits access to quality education and healthcare, reinforcing the cycle of poverty. Progressive taxation redistributes wealth but faces challenges such as tax evasion. State welfare programs like Bolsa Família help alleviate poverty by providing direct support to low-income families, improving social mobility. Countries like Sweden have successfully used similar policies to create a more equitable society. For Brazil, addressing inequality is essential for long-term economic growth and stability, requiring stronger tax enforcement and increased investment in public services.

EIGHT

UNIT 6: INTERNATIONAL TRADE ANDGLOBALIZATION

LEARNING OBJECTIVES

LO1: specialisation at a national level- The basis for specialisation at national level in broad terms of: superior resourceallocation and/or cheaper production methods. advantages and disadvantages of specialisation at a national level for consumers, firms and the economy.

LO2: globalisation- role of multinational companies (MNCs), MNCs and the costs and benefits to their host and home countries. the benefits of free trade. The benefits for consumers, producers and the economy in a variety of countries.methods of protection Tariffs, import quotas, subsidies and embargoes. reasons for protection Including infant industry, declining industry, strategic industry and avoidance of dumping. consequences of protection. Effectiveness of protection and its impact on the home country and its trading partners.

LO3: definition of foreign exchange rate Floating and fixed systems. determination of foreign exchange rate in foreign exchange market. The demand for and supply of a currency in the foreign exchange market and the determination of the equilibrium foreign exchange rate. causes of foreign exchange rate fluctuations. Including changes in demand for exports and imports, changes in the rate of interest, speculation, and the entry or departure of MNCs. consequences of foreignexchange rate fluctuations. The effects of foreign exchange rate fluctuations on export and import prices and spending on imports and exports via the PED. floating and fixed foreign exchange rates The difference between, and the advantagesand disadvantages of, a floating foreign exchange rate and a fixed foreign exchange rate system.

LO4: Current account of balance of payments- The components of the current account of the balance of payments – trade in goods, trade in services, primary income and secondary income. Calculation of deficits and surpluses on the current account of the balance of payments and its component sections. causes of current account deficit and surplus . Reasons for deficits and surpluses. consequences of current account deficit and surplus. Impact on GDP, employment, inflation and foreign exchange rate. The range of policies available to achieve balance of payments stability and how effective they might be.

TERMS TO REMEMBER

1. Specialization at a National Level: Specialization at a national level occurs when a country focuses on producing specific goods or services in which it has a comparative advantage, meaning it can produce them more efficiently or at a lower cost than other nations.

2. Globalisation: Globalisation is the process of increased economic, social, and cultural integration between countries, driven by international trade, investment, technology, and the movement of people.

3. Multinational Companies (MNCs): MNCs are large corporations that operate in multiple countries, producing and selling goods or services across international markets.

4. Host Country: The foreign country where an MNC establishes operations, such as factories or offices.

5. Home Country: The country where an MNC is headquartered or originates from.

6. Free Trade: Free trade is the exchange of goods and services between countries without restrictions such as tariffs, quotas, or subsidies, allowing for increased competition and efficiency.

7. Tariffs: A tariff is a tax imposed on imported goods to make them more expensive, thereby protecting domestic industries from foreign competition.

8. Import Quotas: Import quotas are government-imposed limits on the quantity of a specific good that can beimported into a country within a certain period.

9. Subsidies: Subsidies are financial assistance provided by the government to domestic firms to reduce their costs and make them more competitive in the global market.

10. Embargoes: An embargo is a complete ban on trade with a specific country or on certain goods, often for political or economic reasons.

11. Infant Industry: An infant industry is a newly established industry that may require government protection (through tariffs or subsidies) until it becomes competitive in the global market.

12. Declining Industry: A declining industry is an industry experiencing reduced demand, leading to decreased production and job losses, often due to technological changes or shifts in consumer preferences.

13. Strategic Industry: A strategic industry is an industry deemed essential for national security, economic stability, or public welfare, such as defense, energy, or agriculture.

14. Dumping: Dumping occurs when a country or company exports goods at prices below their production costs to eliminate competition and gain market dominance.

15. Foreign Exchange Rate: The foreign exchange rate is the price of one currency in terms of another, determining how much one currency is worth relative to another in the global market.

16. Foreign Exchange Market: The foreign exchange market (Forex) is the global marketplace where currencies are traded, determining exchange rates based on supply and demand.

17. Demand for a currency: Arises when foreign buyers purchase goods, services, or investments from a country.

18. Supply of a currency: Occurs when domestic buyers import goods, services, or invest in foreign markets.

19. Equilibrium Foreign Exchange Rate: The equilibrium foreign exchange rate is the exchange rate at which the quantity of currency demanded equals the quantity supplied, balancing the foreign exchange market.

20. Exports: Goods and services sold by a country to foreign buyers.

21. Imports: Goods and services purchased by a country from foreign sellers.

Foreign Exchange Rate Fluctuations: Foreign exchange rate fluctuations refer to the rise and fall in a currency's value due to factors such as changes in interest rates, inflation, trade balances, speculation, and foreign investments.

22. Floating Exchange Rate: Determined by market forces of supply and demand, with minimal government intervention.

23. Fixed Exchange Rate: Set and maintained by the government or central bank, often pegged to another currency or a basket of currencies.

24. **Balance of Payments (BOP)**: The balance of payments is a record of all economic transactions between a country and the rest of the world, including trade, investments, and financial transfers.

25. **Current Account of Balance of Payments:** The current account records a country's trade in goods and services, as well as income flows from abroad.

26. Components of the Current Account of the Balance of Payments

a. Trade in Goods – The export and import of tangible products.

b. Trade in Services – The export and import of intangible services like tourism, banking, and insurance.

c. Primary Income – Earnings from foreign investments, such as dividends, interest, and wages.

d. Secondary Income – Transfers such as remittances, foreign aid, and government grants.

27. **Current Account of the Balance of Payments Deficit:** When a country's imports and income payments exceed its exports and income receipts, leading to a net outflow of money.

28. **Current Account of the Balance of Payments Surplus**: When a country's exports and income receipts exceed its imports and income payments, resulting in a net inflow of money.

STRUCTURED QUESTIONS

1. Explain the advantages and disadvantages of specialisation at a national level. [6]

Specialisation at a national level occurs when a country focuses on producing certain goods and services more efficiently than others. One major advantage of this is increased efficiency and higher output, as countries can take advantage of economies of scale and expertise in a particular industry. This leads to greater trade opportunities and economic growth, as countries export their specialized products in exchange for goods they do not produce efficiently. Furthermore, specialisation creates more employment opportunities as industries expand to meet domestic and international demand.

However, there are also disadvantages to specialisation. One major risk is overdependence on a particular industry, making a country vulnerable if demand for that industry declines. Additionally, economies that specialise in resource-based industries may face resource depletion, leading to environmental damage and long-term economic instability. Lastly, reliance on foreign trade for essential goods can make a country susceptible to external shocks, such as global supply chain disruptions or geopolitical tensions.

2. Discuss the role of multinational companies (MNCs) for host and home countries. [8]

Multinational companies (MNCs) play a crucial role in both host and home countries, with significant economic and social impacts. For host countries, MNCs bring several benefits, including job creation and the transfer of advanced technology and expertise. Many developing countries benefit from foreign direct investment (FDI) by MNCs, whichenhances industrial growth and infrastructure development. Additionally, governments benefit from higher tax revenues generated by the activities of these corporations.

However, there are also drawbacks for host countries. MNCs may exploit local labor by offering low wages and poor working conditions. Environmental concerns also arise, as some multinational corporations engage in deforestation, pollution, and excessive resource extraction. Moreover, MNCs may repatriate their profits to their home countries, limiting the economic benefits for the host nation.

For home countries, MNCs contribute positively by generating higher profits and strengthening the economy through remittances from foreign operations. They also improve the home country's balance of payments by bringing in foreign earnings. However, home countries may experience job losses if MNCs outsource production to cheaper labormarkets. Additionally, tax avoidance by MNCs reduces government revenue, as these corporations often shift profits to low-tax countries to minimize their tax liabilities.

3. Discuss whether free trade is beneficial or not. [8]

Free trade refers to the exchange of goods and services between countries without restrictions such as tariffs, quotas, or subsidies. It offers several benefits, including greater consumer choice, as individuals can access a variety of products from different countries. Additionally, increased competition between firms leads to lower prices and higher efficiency, as businesses strive to reduce production costs and improve product quality. Free trade also encourages innovation and technology transfer, leading to higher productivity and economic growth.

However, free trade also has disadvantages. One major concern is job losses in industries that cannot compete with cheaper imports. Domestic businesses may struggle to survive, leading to increased unemployment and economic instability. Overdependence on foreign economies can also be risky, as disruptions in global markets can have seriousconsequences. Moreover, free trade can lead to trade deficits, where a country imports more than it exports, causing economic imbalances. Environmental concerns also arise, as increased transportation and production contribute to pollution and resource depletion.

4. Explain the reasons for protectionism. [6]

Protectionism refers to government policies aimed at restricting imports to protect domestic industries. One key reason for protectionism is to safeguard **infant industries**, which are new and unable to compete with established foreign firms. By imposing tariffs or subsidies, governments give these industries time to grow and become competitive.Another reason is **job protection**, as unrestricted imports can lead to domestic job losses. Protectionist policies help preserve employment in key industries.

Additionally, protectionism helps **reduce trade deficits** by limiting excessive imports, ensuring a more balanced economy. It also prevents **dumping**, where foreign firms sell goods at extremely low prices, undercutting local businesses. Some countries implement protectionism to **secure strategic industries**, such as defense or agriculture, which are vital for national security. Lastly, protectionist measures can help **improve the balance of payments** by reducing reliance on imported goods and boosting local production.

5. Discuss the consequences of protectionism. [8]

Protectionist policies have both positive and negative consequences. On the positive side, they help protect jobs in domestic industries by reducing competition from cheaper imports. Governments can also safeguard national security by ensuring that essential industries, such as food production and defense, remain under local control. Protectionismcan also improve the trade balance by reducing import dependence and supporting local businesses.

However, protectionism also has several drawbacks. One major disadvantage is **higher prices for consumers**, as domestic products may be more expensive than imported alternatives. This limits consumer choice and can reduce overall welfare. Protectionist policies may also lead to **inefficiency**, as domestic firms become complacent without foreign competition. Another major concern is **trade retaliation**, where other countries impose tariffs on exports, leading to reduced global trade. Furthermore, protectionism can slow down economic growth by restricting market access and limiting investment opportunities.

6. What are the causes of foreign exchange rate fluctuations? [4]

Foreign exchange rates fluctuate due to several factors. One key reason is changes in demand for exports and imports—when a country exports more, the demand for its currency increases, leading to appreciation. Similarly, high import levels can lead to depreciation. Interest rates also affect exchange rates; higher interest rates attract foreign investment, increasing demand for the currency.

Another factor is speculation, where investors buy and sell currencies based on expected future movements. If investors believe a currency will strengthen, they buy more of it, causing appreciation. Finally, **government intervention** through central bank policies can influence exchange rates by buying or selling foreign currency reserves.

7. Discuss the consequences of foreign exchange rate fluctuations. [8]

Foreign exchange rate fluctuations have significant impacts on trade and the overall economy. **If a currency appreciates**, imports become cheaper, helping reduce inflation as businesses and consumers pay lower prices for foreign goods. However, appreciation makes exports more expensive, reducing demand from foreign buyers and potentially slowing economic growth.

Conversely, **if a currency depreciates**, exports become cheaper and more competitive, boosting demand and economic growth. However, depreciation also makes imports more expensive, increasing inflation as businesses pay more for imported raw materials and goods. Additionally, foreign debt becomes more expensive if it is denominated inforeign currency. Exchange rate volatility can also create uncertainty for businesses and investors, leading to reduced investment and economic instability.

8. Differentiate between floating and fixed foreign exchange rates. [4]

A **fixed exchange rate** is when a government or central bank maintains a stable currency value against another currency or a basket of currencies. This system provides stability and predictability, making it easier for businesses to trade and invest internationally. However, it requires significant government intervention and foreign currency reserves.

A **floating exchange rate**, on the other hand, is determined by market forces of supply and demand. This system allows for automatic adjustments based on economic conditions, such as inflation and trade balances. However, it canbe highly volatile, leading to uncertainty in international trade and investment. Many economies use a **managed float**, where central banks intervene occasionally to stabilize extreme fluctuations.

9. Explain the causes of current account deficit and surplus. [6]

A current account deficit occurs when a country imports more goods, services, and capital than it exports. One major cause is a high level of consumer spending on imports, which may happen when domestic products are expensive or oflower quality. Another reason is lack of competitiveness, where a country's industries are inefficient or face highproduction costs, making their exports less attractive in international markets. Additionally, exchange rate fluctuationscan affect trade balances—if a country's currency appreciates, exports become more expensive, reducing demand, while imports become cheaper, increasing spending on foreign goods.

Conversely, a current account surplus occurs when a country exports more than it imports. This can be caused byhigh demand for domestic products, strong industrial production, and competitive pricing. A weaker currency also contributes to a surplus by making exports cheaper and more attractive to foreign buyers. Additionally, government policies such as export incentives and import restrictions can lead to a surplus.

10. Discuss the consequences of current account deficit and surplus. [8]

A **current account deficit** can have several negative effects. It often leads to **increased borrowing from foreign countries**, which raises external debt and interest payments. Persistent deficits may also **depreciate the currency**, making imports more expensive and leading to inflation. Additionally, high deficits indicate a reliance on foreign goods and capital, which can reduce domestic industry growth and increase unemployment. However, a deficit is not always negative—it can signal high consumer demand and economic growth if funded by productive investments.

On the other hand, a **current account surplus** can boost a country's economic stability by **increasing foreign reserves**, allowing governments to manage economic shocks effectively. It also strengthens the currency, making imports cheaper and reducing inflation. However, a surplus can also lead to **reduced consumer spending**, as households may not benefit from increased wages or lower prices. Additionally, some countries may accuse surplus economies of unfair trade practices, leading to trade tensions and retaliatory measures.

11. Discuss the policies to achieve balance of payments stability. [8]

To achieve balance of payments stability, governments use various policies. One approach is exchange rate policies, where central banks intervene to control fluctuations. For example, if a country has a deficit, it may allow its currency to depreciate, making exports cheaper and imports more expensive, thus improving the trade balance.

Another method is monetary and fiscal policies—higher interest rates attract foreign investment, strengthening the currency and reducing deficits. Additionally, governments can reduce domestic spending through higher taxes or lower public expenditure to decrease demand for imports.

Trade policies such as tariffs, quotas, and export subsidies can also be used to control trade imbalances by discouraging imports and boosting exports. However, these policies risk trade retaliation from other nations. Lastly, supply-side policies that improve industrial efficiency and productivity can make domestic goods more competitive, leading to higher exports and a more stable balance of payments in the long run.

12. Explain the factors affecting demand and supply of foreign currency. [6]

The demand for foreign currency is influenced by various factors. One key determinant is **international trade**— when a country imports goods, it needs to exchange its currency for foreign currency, increasing demand. Similarly, **foreign investment** affects currency demand; if investors find a country attractive, they will buy its currency to invest in businesses or assets. Interest rates also play a role—**higher interest rates** attract foreign capital, increasing demand for the domestic currency.

On the supply side, a country's **exports generate foreign currency earnings**, increasing the supply of foreign exchange. Additionally, **capital outflows**, such as investors moving money abroad, increase the supply of domestic currency in foreign markets. Finally, **government interventions**, such as central banks selling foreign reserves, can influence the supply and demand of currency.

13. Explain the effects of foreign exchange rate fluctuations on export and import prices and spending on imports and exports via the PED. [6]

Foreign exchange rate fluctuations significantly impact trade. If a country's **currency depreciates**, exports become cheaper for foreign buyers, increasing demand. However, the impact depends on the **price elasticity of demand (PED)**—if exports are **price elastic**, demand will rise significantly, improving the trade balance. If exports are inelastic, demand will not increase much, limiting the benefit of depreciation.

Similarly, depreciation makes imports more expensive, reducing their demand if they are price elastic. However, if imports are inelastic (such as essential goods like oil or medicine), demand may remain high, worsening the trade deficit. Conversely, if the **currency appreciates**, imports become cheaper, increasing demand, while exports become more expensive, reducing demand and potentially harming domestic industries.

14. What are the components of the current account of the balance of payments? [4]

The current account of the balance of payments consists of four main components. The first is the **trade in goods**, which includes the value of a country's exports and imports of physical goods like machinery, oil, and food. The second is the **trade in services**, which covers services like banking, tourism, and education provided to or received from other countries.

The third component is the **primary income**, which includes earnings from foreign investments, such as dividends, interest, and wages earned abroad. Finally, the **secondary income** includes government transfers, foreign aid, and remittances sent by individuals working overseas.

15. State the reasons for deficits and surpluses on the current account of the balance of payments. [4]

A **current account deficit** occurs due to high import levels, often because domestic industries are uncompetitive orconsumer demand for foreign goods is strong. Currency appreciation can also make exports expensive, reducing demand and worsening the deficit. Additionally, high borrowing from foreign countries leads to more interest payments, increasing the deficit.

A **current account surplus** happens when a country has strong export industries, benefiting from a weak currency that makes exports cheaper. Government policies, such as trade restrictions or export subsidies, can also lead to a surplus. Additionally, high foreign investment earnings contribute positively to the current account.

16. Discuss the impact of deficits and surpluses on the current account of the balance of payments on GDP, employment, inflation, and foreign exchange rate. [8]

A **current account deficit** can negatively impact GDP, as it indicates that a country is spending more on imports than it earns from exports, reducing domestic production. High deficits can also weaken the currency, leading to importedinflation as the cost of foreign goods rises. Employment may decline if local industries struggle to compete with foreign firms, leading to layoffs and lower incomes.

Conversely, a **current account surplus** can boost GDP, as high exports increase production and create jobs. Surpluses strengthen the currency, reducing inflation by making imports cheaper. However, excessive surpluses can lead to trade imbalances, causing political tensions with trade partners and potential retaliatory tariffs.

17. Discuss the range of policies available to achieve balance of payments stability and how effective they might be. [8]

Governments use various policies to correct imbalances in the **balance of payments**. One approach is **exchange rate adjustments**—depreciation makes exports cheaper, boosting demand, while appreciation reduces import spending. However, this can lead to inflation if imports become too expensive.

Another method is **monetary and fiscal policies**, such as raising interest rates to attract foreign capital and reduce deficits. However, this can slow economic growth. Governments also use **protectionist measures**, like tariffs and quotas, to reduce imports and support local industries. However, these policies risk trade retaliation from other nations.

Supply-side policies focus on improving productivity and competitiveness, helping industries grow and export more. These policies are effective in the long run but require significant investment. Overall, achieving balance of payments stability requires a mix of short-term and long-term strategies to ensure sustainable trade and economic growth.

CASE STUDY

The Impact of Trade and Foreign Exchange on the Turkish Economy

Turkey is an emerging economy with a diverse industrial base, a growing services sector, and a strong presence in global trade. The country is known for its **specialisation at a national level** in industries such as textiles, automotiveproduction, and tourism. However, Turkey is also heavily reliant on **imports** of energy, machinery, and high-tech goods, which has created economic vulnerabilities.

Due to **globalisation**, many **multinational companies (MNCs)** have invested in Turkey, benefiting from its strategiclocation between Europe and Asia, skilled workforce, and relatively lower production costs. These MNCs contribute to economic growth, employment, and technology transfer but also repatriate profits to their **home countries**, limiting the long-term financial benefits for Turkey.

To protect local industries, the Turkish government has used **tariffs** on certain imports and provided **subsidies** to domestic manufacturers. However, its protectionist policies have sometimes led to trade disputes with key partners in the European Union and the United States.

The country has also faced significant **foreign exchange rate fluctuations** in recent years. The Turkish lira (TRY) hasdepreciated sharply against major currencies such as the US dollar (USD) and the euro (EUR), making imports more expensive and increasing inflation. While the weaker lira has made Turkish **exports** (such as textiles, agriculturalproducts, and tourism services) more competitive globally, it has also made it harder for businesses to repay foreign debt.

Turkey has struggled with a **current account deficit**, meaning it imports more goods and services than it exports. The government has debated whether to allow a **floating exchange rate** or intervene to stabilise the lira. Meanwhile,foreign investors have become cautious due to the high level of **exchange rate volatility** and concerns over economic policies.

Questions and Answers

1-MARK QUESTION:

1. Define a tariff and explain its purpose in Turkey's trade policies.

A **tariff** is a tax imposed on imported goods to make them more expensive. Turkey uses tariffs to protect local industries, reduce dependency on foreign products, and support domestic employment.

3-MARK QUESTION:

2. Identify one benefit and one challenge of multinational companies (MNCs) operating in Turkey.

Benefit: MNCs bring foreign investment, create jobs, and introduce advanced technology to Turkey.

Challenge: Many MNCs repatriate their profits to their home countries, limiting Turkey's economic gains.
4-MARK QUESTION:

3. Explain two effects of foreign exchange rate fluctuations on Turkey's economy.

Increased Inflation: A weaker Turkish lira makes imported goods more expensive, driving up the cost of living and inflation.

Boost in Exports: The depreciation of the lira makes Turkish products cheaper in foreign markets, improving competitiveness and increasing export revenues.

6-MARK QUESTION:

4. Discuss the advantages and disadvantages of a floating exchange rate system for Turkey Advantages:

Automatic Adjustment: The exchange rate changes based on market forces, helping balance trade imbalances.

No Need for Large Reserves: The government does not need to hold vast amounts of foreign currency to maintain the exchange rate.

Competitive Exports: A weaker lira makes Turkish exports more affordable, boosting trade and tourism.

Disadvantages:

Volatility: The lira's frequent fluctuations create uncertainty for businesses and investors.

Higher Import Costs: A depreciating currency makes imported goods, such as fuel and machinery, more expensive.

Foreign Debt Burden: Many Turkish companies have borrowed in foreign currencies, and a weaker lira increases their debt repayment costs.

6-MARK QUESTION:

5. Evaluate the reasons for Turkey's current account deficit and its economic consequences. Reasons for Turkey's Current Account Deficit:

High Import Dependence: Turkey relies on energy and high-tech imports, increasing its trade imbalance.

Foreign Debt: Many businesses borrow in foreign currencies, leading to high external debt payments.

Tourism and Export Variability: While tourism and exports help reduce the deficit, they are affected by global economic conditions.

Economic Consequences:

Weaker Currency: A persistent deficit puts downward pressure on the lira.

Rising Inflation: Costlier imports lead to inflation, reducing consumers' purchasing power.

Foreign Investment Uncertainty: Investors may be reluctant to invest due to concerns

CASE STUDY

The Impact of Foreign Exchange and Trade Policies on the Indian Economy

India, the world's fifth-largest economy, has seen rapid growth in recent decades, driven by industrial expansion, service sector dominance, and increasing integration with the global market. As a major player in international trade, India benefits from **globalisation**, which has facilitated foreign investments, increasedexports, and expanded its workforce. However, challenges such as trade imbalances, exchange rate volatility, and economic dependency on oil imports continue to shape its financial stability.

Multinational Companies (MNCs) and India's Economy

With its large consumer base and skilled workforce, India has attracted numerous **multinational companies (MNCs)**, such as Apple, Toyota, Amazon, and Google. These firms bring technology, employmentopportunities, and capital investment. However, while they stimulate the economy, they also repatriate profits to their **home countries**, causing capital outflows.

India's domestic industries, particularly in sectors like textiles and manufacturing, often compete with foreign firms. To protect these businesses, the government implements **trade protection measures**, such as**tariffs (import taxes), import quotas (limits on foreign goods), and subsidies (financial support for domestic producers).** For example, high tariffs on imported electronics encourage domestic production under the "Make in India" initiative.

Foreign Exchange Rate and its Impact on India

India follows a **floating exchange rate system**, meaning the value of the Indian rupee (INR) fluctuates based on market demand and supply. **Foreign exchange rate fluctuations** impact both consumers and businesses. A depreciating rupee makes imports (such as oil and machinery) more expensive, increasing inflation. However, it also makes Indian exports (such as IT services and textiles) more competitive in global markets.

India's Current Account Balance

The **current account of the balance of payments** records trade in goods, services, primary income (investment earnings), and secondary income (remittances). India has often experienced a **current account deficit (CAD)** because of high oil imports and significant capital outflows. However, earnings from IT exports and remittances from Indians working abroad help reduce the deficit. The government has responded by attracting **foreign direct investment (FDI)**and promoting domestic production to reduce import dependence.

This case study explores how India navigates these economic challenges through trade policies, exchange rate management, and protectionist measures.

Questions and Answers

2-MARK QUESTION:

1. What is a current account deficit, and why does India experience it?

A current account deficit (CAD) occurs when a country's total imports of goods, services, and financial transfers exceed its total exports. India experiences a CAD because: It heavily relies on importing crude oil, gold, and high-tech goods, which increase its import bills. Foreigncompanies operating in India repatriate profits to their home countries, causing financial outflows

3-MARK QUESTION:

2. Identify one advantage and one disadvantage of MNCs operating in India.

Advantage:

Job Creation and Technology Transfer – MNCs provide employment to millions of Indians and introduce advanced technology, improving productivity.

Disadvantage:

Profit Repatriation – MNCs send a portion of their earnings back to their home countries, leading to capital outflows rather than reinvestment in India.

4-MARK QUESTION:

3. Explain two ways in which a weaker Indian rupee affects the economy.

Higher Import Costs: Since India imports large quantities of crude oil, electronic components, and machinery, a weaker rupee makes these imports more expensive, contributing to inflation.

Boosts Exports: Indian goods and services become cheaper for foreign buyers, increasing demand for exports like textiles, IT services, and pharmaceuticals. This helps improve India's trade balance.

6-MARK QUESTION:

4. Discuss the advantages and disadvantages of India using tariffs as a trade policy.

Advantages of Tariffs:

Protects Domestic Industries – By making foreign goods more expensive, tariffs encourage consumers to buy locally produced goods, helping small businesses and domestic manufacturers.

Encourages Local Production – High tariffs on imported products push companies to set up manufacturing units in India, creating jobs and boosting industrial growth.

Government Revenue Generation – Import taxes contribute to government funds, which can be used for infrastructure and social programs.

Disadvantages of Tariffs:

Higher Prices for Consumers – Since imported goods become more expensive, Indian consumers may have to pay higher prices for essential products.

Trade Retaliation – Countries affected by Indian tariffs may impose tariffs on Indian exports, reducing demand for Indian goods internationally.

Reduced Foreign Investment – High tariffs may discourage MNCs from entering India, reducing technological advancements and job creation.

6-MARK QUESTION:

5. Evaluate the impact of foreign exchange rate fluctuations on Indian businesses.

Positive Impacts:

Boosts Export Competitiveness: A weaker rupee makes Indian exports cheaper, increasing demand for IT services, textiles, and pharmaceuticals in international markets.

Growth in Tourism Sector: Foreign tourists find India more affordable when the rupee weakens, leading to higher revenues in hospitality and travel industries.

Negative Impacts:

Increased Cost of Imports: India relies on importing crude oil, machinery, and technology. A weak rupee raises costs, leading to inflation and higher production costs for businesses.

Debt Repayment Challenges: Indian firms and the government with foreign currency loans must pay more when the rupee depreciates, increasing financial strain.

Uncertainty for Investors: Constant fluctuations in currency value create uncertainty for foreign investors, potentially reducing capital inflows.

Bibliography

1. Chandra, R. (2000). *The impact of trade policy on growth in India.*
2. *https://www.cambridgeinternational.org/Images/596945-2023-2025-syllabus.pdf*
3. Herndon, T., & Paul, M. (2020). *A public banking option as a mode of regulation for household financial services in the US. Journal of Post Keynesian Economics, 43(4), 576-607.*
4. Ho, C. Y. (2012). *Market structure, welfare, and banking reform in China. Journal of Comparative Economics, 40(2), 291-313.*
5. Hellwig, M., & Neumann, M. J. (1987). *Economic policy in Germany: Was there a turnaround?. Economic Policy, 2(5), 103-145.*
6. Jaguaribe, H. (1968). *Economic & political development: a theoretical approach & a Brazilian case study. Harvard University Press.*
7. Kanbur, R., & Venables, A. J. (2007). *Spatial disparities and economic development. Chapter, 9, 204-215.*
8. Kirişçi, K., & Kaptanoğlu, N. (2011). *The politics of trade and Turkish foreign policy. Middle Eastern Studies, 47(5), 705-724.*
9. Randall, S. J. (1992). *Colombia and the United States: Hegemony and interdependence (Vol. 6). University of Georgia Press.*